WON'T LET YOU GO
UNLESS YOU BLESS ME

WON'T LET YOU GO UNLESS YOU BLESS ME

A collection of essays

BY
Andrée Seu

printed in the United States of America

Limited First Edition *WORLD Magazine* book, May 2006

Essays in this book were first printed, in one form or another, as columns in *WORLD Magazine,* for which Andrée Seu is a senior writer. Some essays have been revised for this book while others remain as they were originally printed in Andrée Seu's *WORLD Magazine* column.

ISBN 0-9779299-0-6

Book design by *WORLD Magazine*
Cover illustration by Krieg Barrie

Printed in the United States of America
10 9 8 7 6 5 4 3

to Hae Linn, Jae, Calvin, and Aimée

CONTENTS

INTRODUCTION

*February 2006, an e-mail note to the editor
regarding the title of this book*

ONE OF MY FAVORITE places in the Bible is where Jacob says to the angel of God, "I will not let you go unless you bless me."

If that's too long for a title, then how about just "Unless You bless me"?

We could put an amplification just inside the cover, a page with nothing on it but the following: "When the man saw that he did not prevail against Jacob, he touched his hip socket, and Jacob's hip was put out of joint as he wrestled with him. Then he said, 'Let me go, for the day has broken.' But Jacob said, 'I will not let you go unless you bless me'" (Genesis 32:25-26).

I'm a little "out of joint" myself, don't you think? And almost every day I "get violent" with God and say to Him, "I won't let you go unless you bless me."

Que pienses?

—Andrée Seu

WON'T LET YOU GO
UNLESS YOU BLESS ME

A collection of essays

"When the man saw that he did not prevail against Jacob, he touched his hip socket, and Jacob's hip was put out of joint as he wrestled with him. Then he said, 'Let me go, for the day has broken.' But Jacob said, 'I will not let you go unless you bless me.'"

Genesis 32:25-26

AN HOUR AT EVENING

A lament from a wife at her husband's grave

BRADFIELD LIKED TRUCKS, that's for sure. Liked them well enough to have one chiseled into his medium-grade granite—an 18-wheeler no less. Or maybe it was his loved ones who identified the man with the metier, a notion that might seem laughable to the present Mr. Bradfield. But in this world the living prevail.

Funny, though, your being cheek by jowl with a trucker, you who made your living with pen and ink and your companions among the connoisseurs of ideas. Death is the great leveler, is it not?

Want to hear a good one? The groundskeeper tells me about all these headstones with "19__" etched into them and now only seven months to make good on it. A little permutation on the Y2K problem.

What do I do with these flowers, I wonder (I will keep the ribbon: "Loving Husband" "Loving Father").

The succulent reds and yellows of the spray we left for you are now as nondescript as the washed-out, brittle pages of old books, the blossoms being in mid-transformation to the dust whence they came. Which is only right. Why should they survive and you not?

Cemeteries are time warps, I have always felt. Just a quarter mile off the main road, but a pocket of eternity unto itself, the murmuring oaks the only sound, perennial music of the house of mourning.

. . . But for a train that breaks the stillness at 20-minute intervals. Your brother quipped to the graveman that you'd feel right at home here since a railroad slices through our own backyard. It was the first time anyone chuckled in four months.

At the memorial service I told them about the little boy in Chonju in 1962 (I hope that's OK), who crossed out all the multiple choices and penciled in, "All the above wrong. Man not evolved from any animal." You scrubbed the latrine after school for your contumacy, and your Mom was proud.

God's economy is strange. I would never remove a creature so fine, so before the time (There's a giant hole in the universe now). But I am a catechized lady and I know: He it is who fills the shuttle, who plies the loom, and has a billion strands to weave into His tapestry. Here are Rachel and Leah on one level, conniving and competing for Jacob's love.

And when the smoke clears, here is God on another level, and the 12 tribes of Israel standing all in a row. He is building His kingdom. I know it in my head.

Ah, Young, God has fitted His bow with a single arrow and hit not only you, but me, and the four children, and the whole church as well. Because of us the fear of the Lord has fallen on many. Already I hear rumors of wives loving their husbands better, husbands their wives. How the planted seed has sent its shoots out everywhere.

And I would trade all that sanctification just to have you back for one day. But that's because I'm finite and sinful and see but through a glass darkly.

This is the first scribbling of mine that will not fall under your discerning eye. You were the writer, dear, pointing men to Christ for exotic markets in a language I never quite learned, more in the manner of Flannery O'Connor than of Francis Schaeffer. For all truth is God's truth.

Rev. Min says when I feel myself sinking I must start from the beginning: What is true? What is real? God is alive. I am His daughter. You His true son.

Some distance from here a mason is busy inscribing my name next to yours, by my command. Give me a good reason why I should bother to leave here at all before keeping that last rendezvous.

The shadows lengthen. I cannot stay. Peter, James,

and John were not allowed to linger either, remember? Back down the mount for the lot of you, smack into the gritty commotion of sick kids and spirits to be cleaned out. But hide the transfiguration in your heart, that little intrusion of the eschaton. To feed on till the substance of things hoped for can be touched. I will see you again, my darling. And soon.

Andrée Seu's husband, Young Seu, died May 29, 1999.

THE BIG SNOW

Reflections on the blessings of sledding

BECAUSE OF LA NINA, or just because God willed it so (Christians admit no conflict between first and secondary causes), children as far south as North Carolina have been able to sample a northern staple of late. I have imagined them often, cutting out swaths of cardboard, cozying up to the neighborhood kid with the sled, finding the second life of discarded inner tubes, then trudging, with a mission, to the highest hill in town.

The school is closed—the brick and mortar edifice, that is. Classes will be held today in the original one-room schoolhouse, the one fashioned not with human hands, the one God made long before anyone ever thought of herding kids into rigid rows and bolting them in desks, having checked their frogs and rabbit's feet at the door.

Math will be measuring the difference of distance between Billy's toboggan and Vinny's saucer.

Andrée Seu

Science will be stopping to examine a six-pointed crystalline miracle of engineering caught on the mitten. Health class will be experienced instead of learned by rote. Social Studies will be pondering the strange phenomenon of strangers, who never smile as they pass you on the street all year, now waving like long lost friends or comrades in arms.

They say God whispers in our pleasures and shouts in our pain, and maybe this is true, but He is audible enough to me this day, as Aimée, Calvin, and I stake out our course on the summit of Glenside Elementary ridge. I had told Reverend Min when he called to check on me recently that life has simplified itself considerably: "I will live for Him," I said. Min replied, "It's not so much even living for Him, as living in His blessings." It was not a correction but I stood corrected; the pastor's accent was in a better place than mine: What do we render to God, after all? Only trust in Him, and He sends showers of blessings before and behind. Does it get any better than this?

If there is a downside to snow it is also its upside, a grace disguised. Did we say to ourselves, "Today or tomorrow we will go into such and such a town . . . trade and make a profit"? Ought we not to have said instead, "If it is the Lord's will . . . "? Accept God's holiday and stay home. Motorists on the parking lot that is I-95, repent!

I pointed my diminutive companions to the different moods of snow and sky, the pitched tent of the sun, the bridegroom now coming forth from his pavilion "like a strong man, runs its course with joy." I am afraid they will miss it, even one hue or slant of sun. Of course they won't. It will seep in by osmosis and live in dormant memory there, till awakened by a whiff of air one January day in middle age when their own kids tug at coats, breaking some reverie. Right now it's down to serious business: Man your positions, secure the rope, get feet on the steering crossbar, coax the most speed from the hill.

Sledding is the great democratizer. On the slopes no one knows your name, IQ, or proficiency with Windows 98—and no one cares. And those of us for whom the ski havens of the Rockies or even the Poconos are out of reach are not denied the least sensation. How full can you fill a cup, after all? Do the olfactory glands, the retina, the pores distinguish between the expensive Aspen snow and the homegrown kind? And come to think of it, have I not noticed in my own life only the most tenuous correlation between money and enjoyment? The serendipitous rapture of a sublime piece of music on the radio on a drive to the market has betimes surpassed the concert hall.

There is snow because God cannot be contained in one season alone—or one anything alone. He is a lion, a lamb, an eagle. He is shepherd and door and vine. He is the warmth and new life of spring, the rich fruition of summer, the gentle warning of fall, and the promissory slumber of winter. Even Oscar Wilde found the Christ child, at least momentarily, in a snowy landscape, in his children's book, *The Selfish Giant,* and appended this commentary to the ogre's transformation: "He did not hate the Winter now, for he knew that it was merely the Spring asleep." And if snow was the antagonist in C.S. Lewis's Narnia stories, it is only because winter would not give way to spring.

THE NEW MATH

Where quality time is important

I HAVE A DIFFERENT CONCEPT of time than I did a year ago. It's the new math of my life, unexpected perquisite of this unwelcome gift that just keeps giving. The death of a spouse, one learns, is a package that comes full of surprises released one by one. There is the compression of one's life to a small measure, a synopsis visible at a glance, that whole business of a final reckoning. I have new insight into the heightened deathbed lucidity of old Jacob, distilling from his sons' long years their salient, defining deeds. I have seen the Last Judgment ahead of the time.

The lesson of this year is finite numbers: There is a finite number of rainbows you will see in your lifetime, a finite number of full moons—and surprisingly few after all. A finite number of times you will walk into your husband's study and choose to stop and say "I love you," or just brush past for the book you were after.

At first, after he left, I was desperate to live longer, into my 70s at least, just to have a chance to make up for the ungodliness of the first 47 years. But almost immediately I was suspicious of that math—a little too tidy, cut and dry. And felt too much like that old salvation by works rearing its head again. Now I am embarrassed to think that I even entertained the idea of "making up" for things that way.

Here is a game you can play for months: Rake over the past, sift and tinker with it, trying to rewrite just one small part. What a terrible dignity is man's, that his every little word, carelessly strewn, should alter the configuration of the universe for all time—and even have repercussions into eternity.

Still, Paul gives a hint at a more encouraging math, an alien algebra, when he reveals that as by the first Adam's sin death reigned, how much more by the second Adam's death will grace abound. There is something higher than my understanding, then. This is not a zero-sum game.

When I am feeling melancholy I gravitate to ancient cemetery plots. Here is a man who died full of years; here is one who died at 20. But the wind whistles over the one as the other, and there they lie—visited by no one, remembered by no one in the land of the living, as if they'd never strutted their hour upon this stage. "There is no remembrance of former things, nor will there be any remembrance of later things yet to be among those who come after" (Ecclesiastes 1:11). Where is the sting of "untimely" death now? Where is the tragedy of my husband's early passing, from this vantage point two centuries later? What a negligible gain is 30 years more, in the eternal scheme of things. Is this not just Archimedes's theorem applied? "Give me where to stand, and I will move the earth"— and move perspective too.

Thirty years more? Depends what you do with the 30 years, methinks. Was Hezekiah so greatly benefited by the extra 16 he was granted for all his pitiful pleading? Who's to say, but all I know is that those years produced Manasseh, who did evil.

Chechen rebels beating a retreat from Grozny in February threw themselves on Russian landmines, sacrificing life to construct a human footpath for their fellow fighters amidst shouts of "Meet you in paradise!" It was the wrong god, but maybe they had the right idea. It's not the number of summers and winters you pile one atop the other; what an impoverished manner of calculation that is!

And who's to say that 80 mediocre years is better than a four-month season of earnest repentance and seeking after God? What mathematician will produce the proofs for that? How much is the worth of one quiet, unseen act of faith or courage, weighed in the balance against a score of tepid years? Does anyone know the answer to that? Our prayers together got pretty monotonous toward the end: "Lord, when you look at me, do not see me but see the blood of Jesus covering me," we prayed 20 times if we prayed it once.

Jesus died at 33. Where is the man who will say, "Pity, what a tragedy to have been cut down in the prime of life"? Rather, will he not say, "Lord, grant me also a life that short if I will live it to Thee— rather than four score of cycles just marking time." I have one request, that "if I fainting be, Lord let me never, ever, outlive my love for Thee."

LEGGO MY SCRUPLES

*A consumer's lament: What to do when my true feelings
about breakfast foods do not fit inside a checkbox*

IT WASN'T A LIKELY PLACE for temptation, and
she wasn't a likely temptress. I have a cousin who
needs a 12 Step program to stay away from
Bloomingdale's, but that's never been one of my
particular besetting sins. I had made my pickup at
"The Wall" and ridden a half-dozen times up and
down the escalator with a two-year-old, thus fulfilling
the two objectives I'd set out with. I had made it
through the mall without coveting my neighbor's
wealth, or lusting after my neighbor's spouse, and, the
commandments intact, we were heading for the exit.

I saw her from the corner of my eye and sensed
that my election was sure. Clutching a clipboard,
she closed in. "Just 10 minutes of your time, I
promise." And in an exercise of that terrible freedom
that is man's, which philosophers analyze and
psychologists trace to early childhood conflicts, but

which to the rest of us feels like a flip of the coin, suddenly I followed her.

Into the bowels of the three-tiered Behemoth. A sterile cubicle, a table between us. A few screening questions about microwaves and such, to ascertain my middle-classness, and the first task was revealed: to indicate which of a rapid-fire litany of breakfast offerings I'd seen advertised. I was in trouble. Her pencil hovered impatiently over the paper.

"I don't watch much TV," I tried to make a virtue of ignorance.

"That's OK." She was undaunted, not believing the abysmal reality of my condition.

Name after name raced by: "Aunt Jemima's Homestyle Waffles," "Aunt Jemima's Microwave Pancakes," "Kellogg's Common Sense Oat Bran Waffles," "Swanson's Great Starts Budget Breakfast," "Downyflake French Toast," "Downyflake Blueberry Waffles."

People who know great things don't need to be ashamed when they don't know trivia; in fact, it is construed as greater glory to them to be above the fray. But when you don't know the great books, or nursing, or quilting, or American League batting averages, an interview by a breakfast food representative can be a moment of deep personal trauma. I waffled.

Finally I heard it, a glimmer of familiarity in a hostile and uncharted sea. I lunged for the word

Eggo, the name triggering a 1970s TV jingle. My self-esteem was spared for the moment and her survey rescued from implausible whiteness.

But I had spoken too fast. In my enthusiasm, had cut her off in mid-sentence. It turns out there have been refinements since I last tuned in, in the early "Eggo" days when brand and variety were one. "Eggo Nutrigrain Waffles," "Eggo Blueberry Waffles," "Eggo Raisin Bran Waffles."

Too late. I was already committed. How could I break in and ask the poor woman to erase the only circle she'd scored on the page? If she sensed my equivocation, she ignored it and moved on. Page two.

"The reasons that would cause you to buy an Eggo Blueberry Waffle," was the first category.

Uh-oh. We were entering the murky realm of causality. I decided, however, not to share my private, perennial debate as to whether motivation is fundamentally multiple or one.

"'Makes me feel like I'm doing something special for myself' . . . Your choices are: (1) highly probable; (2) probable; (3) good; (4) fair; (5) fairly improbable; (6) highly improbable."

I don't know about other people, but I always get bogged down somewhere between "fairly improbable" and "highly improbable," my emotions, apparently, not capable of as fine gradations as those of the test crafters. Moreover, the choices didn't fit somehow, and the implicit flattery and manipulation in the question was a tad distasteful.

"I don't know," I mumbled.

"Most people stick to the middle when they're not sure," she intoned flatly.

"All right, then, 'Good', No. 3."

"OK." (Circle). "Is convenient."

"Well, convenience is a good thing but . . ."

No empathy was forthcoming from the face across the way.

"Fairly improbable," I pronounced, learning on the spot how bad speeding laws and badly phrased surveys make liars and criminals of innocent people.

"Is appropriate for women."

"What the heck does that mean?"

"It's whatever you think it means."

"(Sigh) Good."

"Is nutritious."

"Probable." (Am I blushing yet? I've never read the list of ingredients on the box, but I suspect the proposition is fairly improbable.)

"Is made for people just like me."

(Meaning?) "Good."

"Is the kind of breakfast I would make if I had the time."

(Problematic premise) "Good."

"Page three, Swanson's Great Starts Budget Breakfast."

"Excuse me, but are these going to be the same questions as on page 2?"

"Yes."

"Look, you're busy and I'm busy. How about we circle 'Good' all the way down?"

My accomplice complies unblinkingly, preferring the unconvincing to the unfinished.

Sensing some ineffable personal stake, I make one last stab at salvaging meaning before going under altogether: "How about just attaching a note stating that nutrition is uppermost for me?"

Maybe somewhere in the Kellogg complex somebody is interested in that comment. And somewhere in a laboratory, an underpaid chemist is worrying about the latest *New England Journal of Medicine* findings on oat bran. But in this room it's all about the survey. More precisely, it's about penciled-in circles and bolting out for lunch.

Ten minutes was the promise and 10 minutes it was. "Thank you. Have a nice day now," she said walking to the door.

"Yeah. Feels like summer today, doesn't it?"

"Yeah, don't forget your bag now."

I picked up my cassettes and my son, and as I rose to leave, I realized that I was capable of anything.

DECLARING INDEPENDENCE √

This literary revolution embraced a dependence upon self

ON WALDEN POND WE STROLLED upon an August afternoon, my sister's family and I, trying to inhale the vapors of Henry David Thoreau, not knowing how much he was already in the warp and woof of us.

We had come to Concord on a lark, to put our steps in his footsteps, and those of Emerson, Hawthorne, and the Alcotts. We had come to fathom the mystery: how so much literary energy had welled up from such a small piece of real estate just northwest of Boston. Was there something in the water?

In New England the steeples of simple, white, wood-framed churches with their apron of grassy commons still serve as bearings for many a town. They are geographical (if no longer moral) compasses in this their second incarnation as tourist guides.

The sign in front of this one is a thumbnail history: The First Baptist Church of Concord. Then, the smaller subscript: Unitarian Universalist. (What tales are left untold in those interstitial spaces!) Underneath, inspirational thought for the week: "I always make the most of what's ahead of me and the least of what's behind me." Inoffensive enough, I suppose. And maybe there's a man in a thousand who will recognize a buried allusion to Paul's words about contentment in Philippians 3:12-14, verses that might once have graced the church board. What in the world has happened here?

The museum just off Lexington Avenue is very informative. For $10 they will tell you how to think about the history of the settlement, of those narrow-minded Calvinists who foisted their religion on the noble Algonquins. It hardly seems like a fair fight: Puritans like frozen specimen under glass vs. museum curators writing the brochures. I inquired for directions to Sleepy Hollow Cemetery.

Grim, rounded slabs crookedly dot the hill like teeth in an old man's mouth. I retrieve a paper from my pocket and jot: "Retire, my friends, dry up your tears. I must be here till Christ appears" (Elizabeth Barrett, d. 1701). A hundred yards and a hundred years up the road, on "Author's Ridge" we read a different ode: "The Passive Master Lent His Hand to the Vast

Soul That O'er Him Planned" (R.W. Emerson, d. 1882).
"He gave his life in service for children and youth"
(Daniel Lothrop, d. 18—).

Do I detect a slippage here? Religion giving way
to poetry? Faith in Christ, subtly, to faith in faith?
Ah, mere anecdotal evidence. To the men's own
testimonies I repair—to books I slighted in school
with these words: "Trust thyself." "No law can be
sacred to me but that of my own nature." "Nothing
can bring you peace but yourself." ". . . [T]he fountain
of all good to be in himself, and that he, equally
with every man, is a door into the deeps of Reason"
(Ralph Waldo Emerson).

There is a saying that heresies are the unpaid debts
of the church. What neglect, then, what crime,
transpired here in Massachusetts, so that Emerson
fired that other shot heard 'round the world, his
declarations of intellectual independence from God?
Why those addresses on "the innate goodness of
man," here in Massachusetts where literature and
education came unhinged from Christianity, and all
on the borrowed capital of the Puritan sermons that
were their school of diction? How is it that grandsons
of the Calvinists are modern-day Unitarians? Oh
"Ichabod," the glory has departed!

In 1838 Emerson addressed the Harvard Divinity
College, without a scintilla of sound doctrine left,

only elegant and naïve claptrap. ("[T]hey have rejected the word of the Lord, so what wisdom is in them?" —Jeremiah 8:9.) In 1909 Harvard shortened its banner from "Truth for Christ's Kingdom" to "Truth," signaling unbounded optimism in man free of God. ("For he flatters himself in his own eyes that his iniquity cannot be found out and hated" —Psalm 36:2.) Connect the dots from Alcott's Plumfield school to Columbine horror.

I also have cocked an ear and listened to Nature. And I can tell you with surety that it doesn't talk back. In the end you are like Frank Asch's bear in *Happy Birthday, Moon*, embarrassed to find that the voice you heard was your echo, the projections of your own desires. General Revelation without Special Revelation is mute, save for the convicting testimony of the deity of the Creator.

On Walden Pond we strolled upon an August afternoon, serene in the knowledge that it belongs to Him. And therefore it is ours (1 Corinthians 3:21), and we will not let them claim it. We listened for a voice and heard more than our own reflections— something breaking through solipsism, a better transcendentalism, an eloquence not blown off like chaff, a dream not washed away like footprints in the sand.

THE LIVING ROOM

*The place where an unlikely pair of fishermen
cast their nets*

TUCKED INTO AN ENDLESS commercial strip—
a Dunkin Donuts, a smattering of real estate agents,
an oversaturation of T-shirt stores, and other Cape
Cod artifacts—was once an unprepossessing family
residence. Unlikely danger. A divine ambush.

It was 1974 by the clock, the winding down of
Nam. Five years after Woodstock and four years
before Jim Jones's Guyana.

That is to say, it was the last sputtering gasps of
bellbottoms, of the omnipresent whiff of illegal
substances, of unbounded terrible possibility.

He was an engineer by trade, she a raiser of
children, five by biology, though it was hard to tell
where her progeny left off and the rest of mankind
began, as I observed the comings and goings in
their house.

I suspect it was her idea, Marge's, this mad

experiment, this hair-brained scheme, as anyone could have told you. For this was Satan's turf, Main Street, Hyannis; and even I, no babe in the woods, upon seeing it at night flashed back to that scariest of childhood memories: Pinnochio riding into Pleasure Island.

No doubt she exercised some sweet persuasion on Joe—something from Luke 12, about wise men discerning not only the weather but their times. Like Joseph in the famine. Like Zerubbabel in captivity. Men who put a finger to the wind and act while the current is auspicious.

The shingle over the door boasted too much—and not enough: "The Living Room." And it may have added underneath, "a coffee house," though I don't recall. In truth it was a few throw pillows and a small coffee machine, Tetley tea in styrofoam cups, and the promise of words of life; and was indeed the Magnusons' living room.

They stumbled in unawares, tie-dyed, stringy-haired twentysomethings, not sensing God's trap, not knowing of their date with destiny. Some turning on their heels at once, others, inexplicably even to themselves, deciding to stay. I, ever on the fringe, and making myself small in a corner, watched night after night.

I had followed the boy from Huemos-sur-Ollon

to this glorified sandbar, having nothing better to do with my life at the end of the 20th century, and already disbelieving for joy (Luke 24:41), though not letting on, scoffer and mocker that I was. I'd insisted on proofs, on my terms, but got back such kinds that transcend logic and made my arsenal of argumentation look like toys in a boy's nursery. I was caught off balance by love, wisdom, some fearful power.

The kid had hitched from Westfield, Mass., in '71, on the lam and out to score hashish and whatever. He scouted out a place to crash. Got a tip—but there was a catch: a night's sleep for a religious head trip. Joe and Marge gave him the gospel, once. He believed on the spot. Spent the next six months on the beach reading the Bible and drinking beer. God polishing His instrument.

It was a parable acting itself out: the down-and-outers, the drunks, the doped up, coming in off the street, out of Pleasure Island. And a solemn threshing going on—the wheat brought into eternal barns, the chaff blown back outside (though how many seeds were sown those nights that sprouted only by some future watering?).

I didn't know about God then, how He likes to do His business, His strange work, with one hand tied behind His back—a middle-aged couple and a ninth-grade dropout, ex-druggie armed with only a Bible and a throw pillow. The whole story of Gideon with a too-big army that needed to be thinned, and thinned some more, the better to make it plain that it is not by might, not by strategy, but by the Holy Spirit.

In the years after The Living Room I forgot about it pretty much, went my way, took a few wrong forks in the road, suffered some—and not necessarily for righteousness.

But in this late summer of my life it comes to me again on a gust of memory, the place where I first saw something like two halves of a circle matching up, something making sense.

And what I most recall, what of everything remains, is Marge standing in her doorway that first day, beaming at a stranger not smiling back, a vagabond, all dirty and dissipated and full of fear.

". . . the wind passes over it and it is gone, and its place remembers it no more" (Psalm 103:16). So let it be—with men and houses all. But be it known that for its brief appointed hour there was a net for catching men, and a tree where the birds of the air came and perched, and whose branches pointed upward, ever upward, and beyond.

OMEGA POINT

———————

What are we working for?

SOMETIMES, IN MID-FOOTFALL, I get confused: am I rushing about my work so that I can eat, or am I eating so that I can work? All this striving, where does it tend to, where is the payoff, the "meaning"? "All streams run to the sea, but the sea is not full; . . . All the toil of man is for his mouth, yet his appetite is not satisfied" (Ecclesiastes 1:7; 6:7). Thus the intellectual pursuit of fractions of seconds at traffic lights, or while removing lint from the dryer lint trap. And then I submerge again beneath the surface of thought into the vortex of quotidian events. Till next time.

God has given man hard labor under the sun. "You load sixteen tons and what do you get? Another day older and deeper in debt." The day trader, in his solitary cubicle, CNBC monitor flickering like an eternal votive flame at the bottom of his screen, is the 21st-century Willy Loman, is he not? One wonders if he will ever emerge from his cell to enjoy his windfall gains. Or if the trading itself has become the thing. It's easy to lose track. What was the goal again?

"Father McKenzie, . . . darning his socks in the night when there's nobody there. What does he care?" Or know? The relentless tide of labor sweeps away all philosophy in its slipstream. This is the last great seduction. Satan may here fold his hands and leave more sensational strategies in his arsenal. Not pleasure, not the red-light district, or the glitter of Trump Palace, but work itself, that mantle of dignity bestowed by God on men, how has it become the rock of stumbling? The people "labor merely for fire, and nations weary themselves for nothing" (Habakkuk 2:13).

I know a man who rises at 5 a.m. and comes home at 10 p.m. He has missed first footsteps, first words, family vacations, anniversaries. I know a man who came to America and made a fortune in the New World; he put his back to the plow. He lived a long life and then he died, and left everything to his sons--who were fools. I see gray suits in restaurants with cell phones in their pockets. They cannot enjoy their dinners but they know it not; they think it is convenient.

All this was grievous to me until I considered . . .

A man in the Russian Gulag had had enough. He decided he'd carried his last stone from pile A to pile B for his tormentors in this Sisyphean farce. He laid himself down to await execution by shovel blade. Just then a fellow prisoner sidled up and, wordless, traced the shape of a cross in the dust; walked away. Aleksandr Solzhenitsyn then gathered himself together and scooped up another rock—this time knowing why.

The rest is history.

"The mass of men lead lives of quiet desperation," quoth Henry David Thoreau. But I know a better quote: Malcolm Muggeridge said the happiest person in the world is the woman who sweeps out her house to the glory of God. She is not aware of the grievousness of her days because she has transcended them with knowledge; she has "overcome" and will receive the hidden manna and also a white stone with a new name written on it, known only to her (Revelation 2:17).

Two women working in a field: One has joy, the other not. What makes them differ who outwardly appear equally yoked? Is it not this, that one keeps her eye on the Omega point, the goal to which all streams run?

Ah, Omega point! And thus am I brought to this happy epiphany one day, only to find (why should I be surprised?) that when I arrive at a new conceptual shore, He has arrived ahead of me. He has anticipated my question and given answer—before I ever had the thought, before I ever breached the womb: "I am the Alpha and the Omega, the beginning and the end," He says (Revelation 21:6). Fix your eyes, o my soul, on the Omega point, and be not unduly bogged down in beta, gamma, and the rest. "Therefore, my beloved brothers, be steadfast, immovable, always abounding in the work of the Lord, knowing that in the Lord your labor is not in vain" (1 Corinthians 15:58).

Scene 1: Willy Loman, working for Willy Loman, walks in, stage right, carrying two large sample cases: *The Death of a Salesman.*

Or imagine: Willy Loman, working for Jesus now, walks in, stage right, carrying two large sample cases: new play.

Andrée Seu

DIAMONDS IN THE SKY

No little stars in the heavenly firmament

WHEN THE TIME COMES that I can't remember who I talked to yesterday, I will still remember the names of Denise Turcotte, Karen Holmes, Gloria Légaré, and Marianne Charette. And if you wheel me up to the chalk-laced edge of a baseball diamond some years hence, I know their ghosts will still appear in the mist, like Shoeless Joe Jackson stepping out from the corn in *Field of Dreams*.

Those were the Nephalim, the giants in the land, in the hard-scrabble Rhode Island town of my youth. Make that the early '60s, before soccer was invented, as far as I knew, and when football was just a tall rumor from somewhere west of Ohio.

If you promise not to tell, I harbor a long suppressed desire to be a 14-year-old boy, but I didn't mind being a girl back then, as long as the Big Four strode the universe, and the *Woonsocket Call* held the presses nightly to learn their glorious summer stats.

The universe consisted, in those days, of your true sandlot field, a dust bowl of a theater, such as are as rare now as metallic diners, drive-in picture shows, and millinery shops. A ball pulled too far to the left could very well have plugged the window of St. Joe's, old textile mill turned elementary school. And what shall we say of the field's complexion— crabgrass not so much mowed as struck periodically with a blunt instrument. It had "character," as they say, in a day when what separated the men from the boys was the defiant grit of teeth in the face of the not-so-random bad hop.

Turcotte was a man in a woman's body, with an arm like a pneumatic drill. She held court over second base, and any other base she had to—plus shallow or deep center field, as the need arose. Holmes, 40 parts talent and 60 parts bulldog tenacity, had honed her craft till she whipped that strike zone into submission. Légaré, great with one hand tied behind her back, rubber in her bat, and a magnet in her glove, looked positively bored with most of the opposition's batting line-up as she made short work of them at first. Charette, a natural phenomenon behind the plate, was Mozart to Holmes' Salieri.

I was the hole in right field, and that only when no one better showed. Most often I collected splinters on the pine wood bench bestriding the first-base line (third base had no seating). Parents stood behind the backstop where my father, having skipped supper, split himself between me and my more gifted brother at Little League.

Boomers came up before the era when all children were "above average" and trophies were dispensed like chewing gum, in remediation of self-esteem problems. We came by ours honestly: wiped out Our Lady of Victories at Ai, decimated Our Lady Queen of Martyrs at Jericho. (Sweetest of all, that last one.)

But it wasn't the glory so much that counted with me, at least not the winning kind of glory. As I think it over in a new century, when the grasshopper looks to drag himself along, and the silver cord is near to severed, and summer belongs to other children, it wasn't about that at all. It was belonging that mattered. The purr of well-oiled machinery, the hum of gears meshing, the being part of a glorious enterprise was what I loved, what I ached for, what pained me dull, like a pebble in the shoe.

A couple of times on visits to Woonsocket I've asked my parents what they're doing now, the Big Four. Three are scattered to the wind, but my father thinks Denise might be a gym instructor at the Mount, which is an answer I accept only since I haven't heard her name on an Olympic roster. And one hopes she's having fun, but I'm pretty sure she'll never have a year like the years of '61 to '65.

Me, I gaze into a summer night sky and, unlike father Abraham, can count the stars. But what he saw is what I picture in my mind's eye, and taste like it's already here: A firmament full of diamonds. A team, all handpicked athletes, where there is no second string and the coach knows you by name. It's in the Bible, I've checked it out just to be sure. No last-minute batting order change if someone better shows up, either.

"And many of those who sleep in the dust of the earth shall awake, . . . And those who are wise shall shine like the brightness of the sky above; and those who turn many to righteousness, like the stars forever and ever" (Daniel 12:2-3).

THE WORD STANDS FOREVER

But it's getting lost in the minds of the biblically illiterate

TOM SAWYER, BRISTLING WITH the largest collection of yellow, red, and blue tickets for the successful recitation of Scripture memorization (tickets he has just got at the schoolhouse door in exchange for bits of lickrish, a fishhook, and other treasures amassed during a certain whitewashing episode) is now called to the podium at the head of the class, which this moment has become the epicenter of the universe, time itself being transfixed and every breath bated and every eye on the improbable scholar and on the Superintendent in his annual descent from on high to bestow the prize: a handsome new Bible.

The question is put to Master Tom by his august benefactor: "Now, no doubt you know the names of all the 12 disciples. Won't you tell us the names of the first two that were appointed?"

And here Mark Twain, out of decency toward his

own creations, tastefully draws the chapter to a close as Tom, unable to slip this caper for all he's worth, for all his blushing and tugging at a button, blurts out: "David and Goliath."

It's supposed to be a funny scene, and someday they will tell you as much in a gloss in the margin, when the last man on earth dies who gets the joke.

We are fast approaching—let us say the handwriting is on the wall—the end of the age of biblical literacy, and the genesis of an age where every biblical allusion will have to be explained—lest ye cast pearls to swine.

I got wind of this in a number of ways, one being *WORLD's* editorial decision, announced about a year ago, to jettison such Christian jargon as "tentmaker" in favor of casting a wider cultural net. And I believe that was right.

WORLD's editor-in-chief Marvin Olasky wrote a column in which he quoted a 1913 *New York Times* article waxing poetic about a new income tax that it compared to a "rock of credit from which abundant streams of revenue will flow whenever Congress chooses to smite it. . . . We may be sure that it will be smitten hard and always harder." I'll bet the man on the street 88 years ago saw Moses in that metaphor, but I wouldn't count on it today.

As the incredibly shrinking cultural Bible repertoire becomes mirrored in the press, contemporary purloined illusions are wont to be more truncated. Some recent citings I have come across include a *Newsweek* essay on the dark side of celebrity titled "Reaping the Whirlwind" (Ah, but does the author really know Hosea?), a Toyota ad with the parsimonious text "Born Again," and again from *Newsweek* a commentary on Hillary Clinton's taste in furniture: "Get thee behind me, Danish modern!"

To be sure, you will still find vestigial language here and there: talk of stumbling blocks, good Samaritans, judging not, walking on water, parting the waters, turning swords into ploughshares, going the extra mile, things not written in stone, Solomonic wisdom, being your brother's keeper, being all things to all men, plagues of locusts, Armageddon, not serving two masters, turning the other cheek, the first being last, the meek inheriting the earth, the patience of Job, houses divided that cannot stand—and other such "shibboleths" in the mouths of people who don't know that "shibboleth" comes from a story in the book of Judges.

And once you've caught on to the fact that our secular pundits bandy about these expressions without a clue as to their origins, you are never quite so intimidated again by Erudition; it's clear that the emperor has no clothes (a saying not from the Bible, by the way).

It just so happens—no lie— that as I was musing on these things, a college friend of my daughter, art major at the University of the Arts here in Philadelphia, called me with an SOS: "Where in the Bible is there something about a flight into Egypt, y'know, as in Giotto's painting by the same name? Gotta know by Monday." We started with a quick briefing on the general division into two "testaments," and never flew much higher than the nitty-gritty of how to write a citation: "Put 'Matthew' and then the number 2, for the chapter, then a colon and 13 dash 18, for verses."

Funny you called when you did, I told Kim. I was just thinking about all the language we're losing these days. Soon we'll be communicating in TV slogans, I guess. But that's not the main thing, Kim. That baby Jesus, the one who fled to Egypt, that's the main thing, that's the part I want you to know. "OK, Mrs. Seu," she said, and thanked me for the help. And I thought I heard an echo of Tom Sawyer.

Andrée Seu

PASSENGER AT THE WELL

———————◆———————

Talking to a stranger on the afternoon train

HAVING MISSED THE 5:20 Lansdale local at Suburban Station by a hair's breadth—and one of those divinely appointed retoolings of schedule that alter all history henceforth—I board the 5:35 R2 to Warminster, an unknown quantity. The amount of humanity that a gaggle of skyscrapers is able to disgorge in 13 extra minutes is something I haven't figured on; there will be no indulgence of hermit preferences on this ride, I see immediately, taking in at a glance the long corridor of double seats all systematically staked out at half occupancy, like some perfect binary math exercise of schoolboys.

This is the Northeast megalopolis, not Southern hospitality; our mothers all taught us not to talk to strangers and it's the only remnant of propriety we adhere to. Greek moniker notwithstanding (philos = "love"; adelphos =

"brother"), each commuter is hermetically sealed in his slot.

The first available haven is with a business woman, her overstuffed bag plopped down in the leg room of the adjacent space like a hostile takeover, or a "keep out" sign. This is not to be. I move on.

Directly behind is a fortyish man in a suit who is already looking in my direction and has cleared away his briefcase. I make an instant calculation, factoring in the gravitational pull on my parcels against the likelihood of other prospects, and timidly venture: "May I?" "First woman who's ever sat next to me," he says. "Let's celebrate," I say, surprised at myself, and releasing my bulging canvas bag with a thud. (The lady in front of us chuckles, sneaking a peek over the top of her seat.)

Well, that went as well as could be expected, I muse, settling in. In the enforced silence of Northern train culture I suddenly think of John 4 and the woman at the well. No doubt greater theological depths are to be plumbed in that pericope, but at the moment I am thinking of Jesus the taboo-breaker, striking up a conversation with a person He shouldn't, in a place He shouldn't.

Two nuns appear in our compartment now, donning flying buttress headgear. "I haven't seen veils like that since before '65 and the Second Ecumenical Council," I say, trying to keep up the momentum, and sending out a probe. "They're old," he replies, not revealing much. "I guess they're pro-choice about dress," I say. He nods. I have my wedge into conversation.

I can't recall exactly how but we establish, before the Fern Rock station, a common pedigree: lapsed Roman Catholicism. For him, the end of the line; for me, the beginning. He recounts an encounter with a bunch of people he met out West who think you have to be "born again." I tell him he probably has to throw me in that kettle too. "John 3:16," I reference, cementing solidarity with the Western weirdos. And then I elucidate, "Y'know, all those subversive signs you've spotted in baseball bleachers."

"All kinds of saviors out there these days," he says. "Before you know it, you're drinking Kool-Aid laced with arsenic." "That's why you have to read the Bible," I urge, trying in one fell swoop to set ground rules for epistemology. "The Bible prophesied about all those weirdos. . . . Do you have a Bible?"

My companion at this point makes a detour into abstractions, woman-at-the-well-type digressions, as it seems to me: God as a benign cosmic force and not a person. The usual. But I'm not going down that road; it's a black hole and we don't have the time. "If God hasn't spoken into space and time, it's all opinion anyway," I say, cramming all I know of Francis Schaeffer into a nutshell. "Personally, I work it from the center, not the edges. The most immediate data in the universe: my sin." And here I confide (because he seems interested), "If every thought I had, just this week, were written down in a book, I'd hate for anyone to read it."

"I would too," he says, in a breezy statement that confirms 4,000 years of Scripture tradition, and I marvel that you can park yourself near anyone on any train and the gospel will hit the nail on the head every time.

"Do you like your job?" I query some miles later. "Parts," he says, disclosing his occupation as chiropractor, and I am suddenly aware of sitting next to a guy who shells out maybe $200,000 a year in malpractice insurance. "Come to me, all you who are weary and burdened, and I will give you rest," I sigh inwardly.

The conductor calls out Jenkintown—a kilometer and a tax bracket away from the next stop, mine. And as the man in the suit smiles and disembarks, I hope some gospel pollen brushed off my sleeve, some mustard seed, perhaps, that another will water, in another train, another time. "Hey, chiropractor from Jenkintown, Jesus is pursuing you!"

I have the whole seat to myself again, the way I wanted. Dinner, next on the agenda, will be a half hour late tonight, but I feel strangely sated. And if the chuckling lady in the seat in front hadn't gotten off at Elkins Park, she would have heard the 2,000-year-old sentiment that percolated to my lips just then: "I have food to eat that you know nothing of."

VANITIES, VANITIES

A postmodern evangelism primer

WHEN FRANCIS SCHAEFFER WROTE *The God Who Is There*, the book that escorted me into the kingdom in 1974, he spoke of a chasm between the generations brought about by a change in the concept of truth. That chasm is pretty much closed now. It's likely that your mother, your geriatric hairdresser, and the pastor of the mainline church down the road have all become part of the philosophical shift that was once claimed only by the hippies who roamed his Alpine home. When I told the woman next to me on the plane to Asheville, North Carolina that I was a Christian, she thought that was "sweet." It was no threat to her—whether she be Buddhist or Unitarian. All truths are equivalent. Antithesis is dead. (Give me the good old days before Hegel, when fist fights would have broken out at this point as the lady understood me, correctly, to be saying: My way is true; your way is false.)

A day later, at the World Journalism Institute conference, it was brought to my attention that most Christians couldn't articulate their worldview if their lives depended on it. This was not altogether surprising to me since I have the same problem. During a break I privately asked a speaker for a few one-liners to share on the plane ride home, but she smiled and said, "You want the 'four spiritual laws' for postmodern evangelism?" It sounded like a rhetorical question so I didn't say yes, though that's exactly what I wanted. I knew I had to do some thinking.

There was a time I could spin a pretty good worldview. With Nietzsche and a few other God-is-dead books in my knapsack, I had turned my back on bourgeois morality and my face to seeking the adventure that I believed Fate would hand me. You'd think my parents would be proud of such consistency to my presuppositions, but they just kept bringing up the $12,000 they had spent on college tuition. (Definitely people on the other side of the chasm.)

Swiss L'Abri seemed as good a place as any to start suffering the meaninglessness of existence, so I honored a promise to my brother Marc and made my way to Chalet les Mélezes, where I told Mr. Schaeffer to his face (and over his wife's cooking) what I thought of his Christianity: There was no way to know anything about truth or God starting from your own mind—and that's the only place we can start!

Turns out he had heard that one before. He even had a name for it—"Rationalism"—that distinguished it from "rational," which he believed Christianity to be. The "-ism" thing was older than Plato, and had run out of steam a while back as history was littered with its corpses—all the guys you've read about in Philosophy 101 who'd tried, building out from their own reason, to draw a circle that would encompass all of reality. (Aquinas was purportedly the culprit here, disseminating the mischief that while man's will was fallen, his intellect wasn't.) One weary day philosophers woke up and decided they weren't going to find that circle, and then there was a collective "so now what?"

If you have seen Samuel Beckett's 1955 play *Waiting for Godot*, you will know that when people reach the exit of "despair" on the highway of life, they still have to keep driving; life doesn't just end, however anticlimactic that may feel. You make conversation. You sing a little doggerel. You do a little dance. You fight and make up: It passes the time.

As tip No. 1 in your postmodern evangelism primer, for your next plane trip, it's a safe bet that the fella you'll be yoked with for three hours lives below what Schaeffer calls "the line of despair." This means he has no real meaning in his life. It doesn't mean he'll be weeping into his peanuts, because chances are he doesn't know he lives there, so full is his life with the little "Godot" type distractions. Maybe he is a businessman who tells himself, as did the hopeless Middle Ages Stoics, "Be worthy of your beard." Perhaps she is a housewife, ever rational (and disdainful of Christian "irrationalism") who escapes into a Harlequin romance because the existence of Romance gives her hope (a total "leap" from her more honest determinism) that somehow, somewhere, there is meaning.

You will do better than I did en route to Asheville. You will lend her a hand out of despair by saying that God is there, that He is personal and infinite and has spoken into the circle, that man is guilty but still has worth, and that this isn't "your" truth but "the" truth. And if she has been appointed unto eternal life, your words will not return to you empty.

IN DUE TIME

Looking beyond tragedy—with confidence

WE HAVEN'T SEEN ALL the fallout of this yet. After a stretch of smooth sailing that I mistook for wellness, the child has taken to bedtime queries about orphans—with more than a theoretical interest. This isn't out of the blue, it is on schedule, I suppose: the next phase, a time-released installment of mourning, side effect number 57 of having your daddy ripped from you.

I know what you're wondering, little one: Where are the promises? You cry in the night but . . . silence. We have to talk about "time," you and I. My years are more than yours, you know. Not to pull rank, but at 7, patterns hardly begin to emerge. Still, you may have noticed in our Bible stories, the way it feels long between promise made and promise kept. Abraham. Noah. Old man Simeon.

People fall into that time trap, Aimée. They think God forgets, or God is distracted doing something else—and they do anything they please. Cause and effect get all confused for them and they say silly things like: "But we will do everything that we have vowed, make offerings to the queen of heaven and pour out drink offerings to her, as we did, . . . For then we had plenty of food, and prospered, and saw no disaster. . . . What is the profit of . . . walking . . . before the Lord of hosts?" (Jeremiah 44:17-18; Malachi 3:14). It's true, they get it upside down, even smart people—mathematicians and presidents.

Someday your big brother will teach you chess, and that will help. Till then, remember Joseph of the psychedelic coat? How sometimes things that start out bad turn good, and things that start out good turn bad? You and I read about that little Jewish boy's peaks and valleys in a single sitting, from our catbird seat in history. But what about him, Aimée? (I know you're good at imagining.) What did he feel like in that caravan of Ishmaelites?

Let's play this out; how are you at seeing around corners: hated by your brothers, sold like an old Beanie-baby, orphaned like a kitten, a teenage slave. Isn't that bad, darling?

No, it's good! He ends up the household manager of Pharaoh's captain of the guard!

Isn't that good, Aimée? No, it's bad: Potiphar's wife frames Joseph and he lands up back in jail.

Isn't that bad, Aimée? No, it's good! In jail, he hears important dreams that land him as Pharaoh's vizier. Strands of history and geography woven together by a skillful hand, and Joseph saves his dad and brothers, and counts his former troubles but a pittance on the scales.

"Better is the end of a thing than its beginning" (Ecclesiastes 7:8). The last chapter is what counts, isn't it? Between the covers of the book, knights will fall, pawns will be sacrificed, bishops will topple and be toppled, rooks will come and go—all those great upheavals and reversals Mary saw in the Spirit, singing her Magnificat.

The faithfulness of God is why the perseverance of man (and little girls) is so important. What you're seeing now is middles, freeze frames, the crest of the curve and not its falling arc, the ball as it looks snapped in mid-air by your Polaroid. But "you have heard of the steadfastness of Job, and you have seen the purpose of the Lord, how the Lord is compassionate and merciful" (James 5:11).

There will be magic, daughter mine (I know you are a big girl and you understand). Remember Sleeping Beauty, how the fairies' wands turned arrows of the witch's archers to daisies in mid-flight? Think of it like that. God will turn your hurt to joy, and the Valley of Achor to a door of hope.

Too early to call this tragedy, my girl. Not a forever-after one, at least. A farther seeing eye, before the sun had ever run its maiden course, determined the exact time and place for you, that you might seek Him, and it was in this family (Acts 17:26-27). No slip-ups.

We haven't seen all the fallout of this yet, the gentle misting rain of grace. Of a love and power that more abounds where sin and tragedy abound. Neither the precipitation of Adam's sin, nor of the Second Adam's triumph over it, has all been tallied up to date.

So wait on the Lord, little one, wait. Because of the promises. Because "the proper time" He will lift you up (1 Peter 5:6). Because His compassions are new every morning. Because He is good to those whose hope is in Him (Lamentations 3:25). Wait on the Lord, child, and be still. Because we haven't seen all the fallout of this yet.

DEPTH PERCEPTION

———————◆———————

Loss of a spouse is also loss of a perspective

THERE IS A THREE-LEGGED cat in my neighborhood. As far as I know, his only sin was to be born too close to the railroad tracks. Moses (his name) lives two houses down from me, so every now and then, if we're both setting out for the day at the same time, our eyes will meet and there is a moment of recognition—the feline with a hind leg missing, and that other amputee, sans spouse. Then the fat gray tabby lumbers off to do whatever a three-legged cat can still do when his bird-catching days are over, and I do the same.

A straight shot through the core of the earth, a one-eyed mongrel named Pangouri lies tethered to a corrugated tin-roofed cottage in the rice paddy village of Puan, victim of an untoward impulse to veer too close to a mother and her pups. The odd thing is that his master (my father-in-law) also lost the sight in one eye not long after his son (my husband) died.

Some people think there was a connection. In any case, I heard he had a little fender-bender soon after that, which did not surprise me one bit since, whatever Korean driving laws allow, I know that you really need two good eyes on the road for depth perception.

Depth perception is the single biggest thing I miss in marriage. You can keep your Saturday night movie dates and the other perks of matrimony; I can live without them all. What causes me to lumber about and walk into walls these days, however, is the forfeit of a perspective other than my own. If personalities are colors, I see indigo and my husband always saw yellow—which is the reason I married him in the first place. Together we could be a good start toward a rainbow. We could be "thesis / antithesis / synthesis," and on a good day, "iron sharpening iron." Alone I am a cyclops.

Notwithstanding a fashion among movie starlets like Jodie Foster to opt for who-needs-a-father parenting, what I see is multi-perspectivalism even in the Trinity (Genesis 1:26; 11:7; Proverbs 8:22; Acts 2:33-35). Reality is profoundly relational and collaborative.

Even Moses (the other one) had to be rebuked by his father-in-law for the hubris of thinking he could judge every case by himself; I understand he got 70 men to help. OK, he had 1 million litigants to adjudicate for and I have only four, so I should not exaggerate my problems. But it's a good principle Jethro had there: "What you are doing is not good .... look for able men ... men who fear God .... So it will be easier for you, and they will bear the burden with you" (Exodus 18). And what's good for Judges is good for private citizens too ("Two are better than one ... if they fall, one will lift up his fellow .... Again, if two lie together, they keep warm .... though a man might prevail against one who is alone, two will withstand him"(Ecclesiastes 4:9-12).

The headwater of this stream of one-anothering is Genesis 2:18, of course: "It is not good that the man should be alone"—which is quite a thing to say, considering that no less a One than God Himself was with him all the time!

To be sure, there is always the church—expanded mutuality—and I'm lately keen on claiming doctrine about membership in that body of Christ. But life is not tidy. The best questions and worst crises come at 2:15 a.m. It's those powwows I miss, when I woke the man beside me with urgent queries that couldn't wait till morning, like "Do you think Jeroboam's little boy was saved?" By breakfast time the crisis is past and the issue forgotten, or at least it would require considerable motivation to dredge it up again and look up some elder's phone number.

My husband, with that other set of chromosomes of his, would no doubt frown a bit over my words and bid me tweak this essay's lament (indigo) into an appreciation (yellow), find the nugget of encouragement in the dung pile, polish it up, and then send it off for Valentine's Day and not for Maundy Thursday. That's marriage at its best.

And so, in his honor, here is my "cup half full," a *post facto* marriage appreciation, and a looking forward in faith to the Age of Completeness, when "No more shall there be in it an infant who lives but a few days, or an old man who does not fill out his days" (Isaiah 65:20), or wedding banquets that run out of wine, or limbs that hang limp and useless, or widows and three-legged cats.

TRIANGULAR TRUTH

Why good journalists are hard to find

I WOULD SUMBIT TO YOU that knowledge has a shape and that it is triangular (See John Frame, *The Doctrine of the Knowledge of God*). This would be of interest to all, I should think, but I have in mind in particular those who aspire to be writers, those Bezalels of word-crafting for the kingdom of God. Therefore, as I am helped by the humble triangle in visualizing what I'm up against in putting pen to paper, I have just enough effrontery to think it may benefit another.

Call the three angles God's law, the world, and one's self (or, to make it fancier, the "normative," "situational," and "existential" perspectives, respectively). What is important to note here is that we are pretending, for pedagogical reasons, that knowledge can really be separated out like that. In fact, you will never encounter, in the wild, a "situational" running around without a "normative" or an "existential"—by which I mean nothing more than John Calvin did in his opening words of the *Institutes*, where he declared that to know God you must know yourself, and to know yourself you must know God. There will be overlapping, and a broadening of each angle to include the other two.

Think of a flashlight. You appreciate its light only as it illumines the stray sock or wayward homework assignment under your bed. Likewise, God's law in Scripture edifies as you see it give definition to your world—you read that a "soft tongue can break a bone" (Proverbs 25:15), then one fine day you observe a wise woman defuse a potential catastrophe with a soft answer to an incendiary remark. You observe the downward spiral of a neighbor ensnared in adultery, and then belatedly remember the prophecy, "many a victim has she laid low, . . . Her house is the way to . . . the chambers of death" (Proverbs 7:26-27). And so we find reciprocity: The more you know about the world, the better you understand Scripture. Life illumines Scripture as Scripture illumines life. Behold King Solomon, knower of God's mind, botanist, and wildlife expert (1 Kings 4:33).

The Christian writer has it all over the non-Christian writer on the "normative" angle—in so far as he is consistent to his profession of faith, that is. As Moses exclaimed, "What great nation is there, that has statutes and rules so righteous . . . Keep them and do them, for that will be your wisdom and your understanding in the sight of the peoples" (Deuteronomy 4:6-8). We have a secret weapon—the truth—and are heady as the man in Matthew 13 who found hidden treasure in a field. Meanwhile, your counterparts in the big news rooms scramble frantically to find facts ("situational")—and then have no framework of truth ("normative") to plug them into, something they then try to conceal by their talent ("existential") for stringing words together. Like the Blind Men and the Elephant of the John Godfrey Saxe poem, one mistakes the trunk for a snake, the other an ear for a fan, the other its tail for a rope, and so on, all of them missing the pachyderm!

The Christian journalist is not naïve and is not caught by surprise. "Follow the money" is a tip right out of our playbook on the depravity of man, and should not be credited to Woodward and Bernstein's secret Watergate source "Deep Throat" as if it were original to him. The assiduous acquisition of Scripture knowledge ("normative") hones our intuition ("existential") about what's really going on. Trust your Bible-honed instincts, then check them out with the facts ("situational"); it's a reciprocal dance. And remember too that "facts" ("situational") may not always be as firm as they at first appear (remember the "Piltdown Man"?), nor "instinct" as flimsy—especially "instinct" that is the distillation of a thousand "quiet times."

Finally, if our triangular analysis is right, one corollary would be that knowing the Bible is not enough to be a journalist (no more than it was for Bezalel to be the architect of the Tabernacle). Who will write a helpful column on the Arab-Israeli conflict? Neither the one who knows only Scripture nor the one who knows only Middle Eastern history but the one who is versed in both. The richest writing (the writing I envy) draws from a wealth of knowledge from various spheres. I once heard Frank DeFord, senior writer for *Sports Illustrated*, do a radio essay on baseball's shrinking strike zone, and the crazy guy made allusions to metaphysics and Shakespeare's *Hamlet*!

Every writer on the planet has strengths and weaknesses that fall differently on the normative, situational, existential triangulation; and if anyone possessed all three to perfection, there'd be no living with him. Nevertheless, wise is the wordsmith who recognizes the importance of the triangle and does his best to sharpen each angle. He will be a "workman approved by God" indeed.

CHRISTMAS CONNECTION

If there are no Ramahs there is no need for Jesus

ON THE NIGHT JESSE FELL I was starting to be concerned about Christmas. Oh, not about the story in Matthew 1 particularly, but about how I was going to see my way, on this year's budget, to buying presents for rich people who already have houses full. Jesse put an end to this when she somehow let her body drop from a 30-foot bridge onto macadam about a mile from here in November. The police are investigating.

Jesse came to live with me and my two youngest in September, a high-school friend of my older daughter, and an art student just back from a year in Rome and needing a credible address so as to pursue studies in the university 10 minutes from here. (Her father lives an hour away, and her mother three hours.) I offered Hae Linn's old room and told her straight out that I wasn't much of a hand-holder or friendship material, being occupied enough with my family's own survival and all. She was 21, she could come and go as she pleased, raid the fridge, and generally make herself at home. I kept her in homemade granola, which I noticed she relished.

It is amazing that Jesse survived, let alone that she choked up my phone number when they found her oozing blood from the head. Detectives at the scene called here to get her parents' phone numbers, before volleying questions about mental health, to which, of course, I pleaded ignorance. Memory groped hurriedly through shards of recent conversation, not so much for them as for me, to learn what I already feared to learn, both about Jesse and myself.

I am momentarily in love with the medical profession, with a neurologist and trauma doctor especially, who met us in the waiting room an hour later, looking stern and painting every bleak scenario— as was their duty. But, by the light of morning, they had slain each medical Hydra and Chimaera and brought better news than anyone deserved to expect. The next day they'd tackle the femur, and the next day a scattering of broken vertebrae with awful names like T-12.

The first one I phoned before rushing to the hospital was Leslie, a once-a-year-maybe contact who has been praying for Jesse's salvation for ages, Jesse hailing from what is often called a "not religious" family, though of course there's no such thing. It was perhaps four years ago that Leslie and Jesse sparred in my kitchen, human proxies of a much larger battle, Leslie flinging across the room, in tones more usually reserved for threats, "I'm going to pray for you!"—and Jesse flinging back, "Don't you dare!"

The Lord does as He pleases, and without a doubt the Lord led Jesse to my house, not Leslie's, but it doesn't mean we can infer anything. In the three months we shared a roof I had sensed the pressures and deep waters, and tacked the girl onto the end of my prayer list. On the rare occasions that we did speak, I dispensed mealy-mouthed counsel you could have pulled from any self-esteem handbook at Borders. I was working up to sharing Christ, but it wasn't the right time to pop the gospel yet.

"The little Lord Jesus asleep on the hay." Whatever happens to Jesse, Dec. 25 will surely come, with presents galore and songs of the sweet babe of Bethlehem. Carefully quarantined from this heart-warming tale will be images of those other babies hacked to death in neighboring Ramah: "Rachel weeping for her children; she refused to be comforted, because they are no more." Hatred. Jealousy. Selfish ambition. Death.

But the Lord, who is not so sentimental, has

placed Matthew 2 after Matthew 1, for the reason, I presume, that we should make connections. If there are no Ramahs there is no need for Jesus. If there are no young women who fall off bridges, no middle-aged women with calloused hearts, then what is the point? If Jesus' incarnation was not "to destroy the works of the devil" (1 John 3:8), then what was it for? The baby in the manger is a scene without a plot, good news without the bad, nonsensical. Jesus is cute, ornamental, warm and fuzzy—and ultimately irrelevant.

The fall of Jesse and the birth of Jesus have this one thing in common, strangely enough: They both introduced a crisis. Half-heartedness is untenable, the time for double-mindedness is over, and decision is imperative. Things are suddenly sharp and clear. And as that old unsentimental Jew Simeon dared to put it, at the risk of holiday political incorrectness, "the thoughts from many hearts will be revealed" (Luke 2:35).

A LONG, SLOW FAST

*Mutinous thoughts arise during
a difficult spiritual discipline*

ON SUNDAY THE CHURCH ASKED us to fast the coming Tuesday, which I forgot to do, and so I decided to do it Wednesday, hoping it would count towards the collective effort all the same, and that there was not some mystical necessity breached by the 24-hour lag.

We moderns seem to be clueless about fasting, all of us standing around looking at each other to see if the other guy knows what to do. I remember that in seminary years ago when a day of fast was declared, you would see those guys around 6 p.m. fairly salivating and queuing up at the supper bell like drooping huskies after the Iditarod, which to me was a very wimpy fast, for I was fresh out of a tradition where fasting was fasting, and meant the entire day, not this business of skipping breakfast and lunch. I went the whole three meals back then in Bible school—and was mighty proud of it too.

On the other hand, the Arabs, who are much tougher than I am, fast only till sundown, which is getting me thinking again; maybe the seminary boys had the right idea.

As far as I can tell, the purpose of fasting is that every time your stomach growls, when you would naturally raid the fridge, it reminds you to pray, which is not something that comes naturally otherwise. Plus, fasting makes you thankful for food in general— if you can get over your initial ill will towards the ingrates around you who are stuffing themselves like it's their inalienable right. By evening you are feeling amazed and grateful to be living in America, and you can hardly believe your good fortune that tomorrow morning you will walk down to the kitchen and have pancakes with real Vermont syrup.

About 10 a.m. I decide to make tea. I never drink the stuff, always finding it a waste of time when there's orange juice or chocolate milk or other more substantial beverage around. But I remember this "Celestial Seasonings" I saved in the cupboard for company; and tea is just water, I figure, and you're allowed to have water on a fast, right? But now I start wondering if that's cheating, and if Satanic thinking is taking hold, in my vulnerability, to mess up my fast. Is it a sin to get a little peach flavor in my water when I'm supposed to be denying myself?

The behaviorist benefit of the fast is working, at least. Like Pavlov's dog with religion, I get in the habit of praying at every unpleasant surge of gastric juices. A string around the finger would do the same, though, so there must be some spiritual dimension about which I'm uneducated.

The materialist in me rears its head around noon, after having been presumed long dead: Is anything really accomplished, any peg moved an inch in the universe, by my not putting toast in my mouth today? And am I not in fact merely trying to manipulate the Almighty with this glorified hunger strike?

Come early afternoon I detect the mutinous thought that I won't be any good to my kids if I'm near fainting, and that it's more important to get my work done than not to eat something; and in any case my attitude has been so mixed that I have surely already blown whatever spiritual benefit would have accrued to my self-affliction . . . . Also, I pray for the church.

The terrible thing about being a Christian is that you don't have to do anything for salvation. You don't have to sell your possessions and give to the poor. You don't have to be a missionary. You don't have to live in a house below your means so that you'll have more money to invest in the poor. You don't have to seek the Lord wholeheartedly like Hezekiah (2 Kings 18:3). You can seek him but not wholeheartedly, like Amaziah (2 Kings 14:3). And you don't have to fast.

Thursday, 4 a.m. now, and I know this: I am dust. There are only a few meals between me and death. I am utterly dependent on God's good pleasure for my very existence.

David fasted when he was in trouble (Psalm 69). Jehoshaphat called a fast when the Moabites came up against him (2 Chronicles 20). Ezra fasted to ask for safe passage (Ezra 8:21). Esther would not go to the king unless a few fasted with her (Esther 4:16). Joel proclaimed a fast for backslidden Israel to repent and ward off disaster. And till I understand a lot of things better—like how prayer affects eternal decrees, how suffering produces character, and why it is we fast—that will be good enough for me.

'TIS THE SEASON

*We're probably stuck with the excesses of Christmas,
but we can still turn holiday tradition to
the advantage of the kingdom of God*

I AM HAVING SECOND THOUGHTS about my "Let the dead bury their own dead" Christmas attitude. Last year's essay took a swipe at rich people gifting other rich people. Immediately thereafter, lavish expressions of seasonal love came flooding my way—from people who either don't read *WORLD* or who forgave me.

A C.S. Lewis Christmas anecdote: "My brother heard a woman on a bus say, as the bus passed a church with a Crib outside it, 'Oh Lor! They bring religion into everything. Look—they're dragging it even into Christmas now!'" (*Letters to an American Lady*).

I understand that there are churches that do Christmas to the hilt, and there are others that religiously ignore it, bending over backward not to do anything different on December 25 than December 26 or the second Tuesday in July. Between the polarizing extremes of human conviction, one can often count on God coming up with a third way that we will all find breathtakingly simple when it is revealed on Judgment Day.

This Christmas curmudgeon, who by temperament hates shopping malls and experiences the four weeks after Thanksgiving as a tightening vise, has come to a *via media* between rejecting Christmas entirely (they tell us it would wreck the retail economy) and a whole-hog embrace. This proceeds from the sobering realization that the strands of Christmas, like the holiday wreath, are by now so twisted together, the good with the bad, that to uproot one would be to injure all. (The servants asked the man who had planted good seed in his field if they should pull up the weeds the enemy had sown. "But he said, 'No, lest in gathering the weeds you root up the wheat along with them.'" [Matthew 13:28-29].)

What are the strands worth saving, and pruning?

Since in all matters it is prudent to consider the degree to which humor shapes opinion—in John Frame's terms, how the "existential" colors the "normative"—I took my tirade to a more sanguine friend for her perspective (she loves God and loves malls). Together we decided that like it or not, we're stuck with Christmas. A wise man deals with reality as he finds it. A wise man finds a way to take the givens of culture and turn them to advantage for the kingdom of God. Do the Athenians have a statue to an unknown god? Fine, let's talk about it. Do Americans have a tradition of celebration toward the end of the calendar year? Fine, let's see what we can do with this raw material.

Folks who haven't darkened a church door in years get warm and fuzzy about playing Christmas carols in December. Good. Play those carols round the clock, saturate the airways, take back in free air time the publicity for the gospel that the courts are taking away with the other hand as they nit-pick the Pledge of Allegiance and yank Ten Commandments plaques from judges' offices. You say they like "Silent Night" and "God Rest Ye Merry, Gentlemen" only for the tunes and not the words? So what? They get the lyrics free whether they would or not. Let it get under their skin: "Christ the Savior is born," "to save us all from Satan's pow'r when we were gone astray, O tidings of comfort and joy."

Pauline strategy: "Conduct yourselves wisely toward outsiders, making the best use of the time" (Colossians 4:5). Make a list of people who would find you weird if you did something nice for them any other time of the year but would find it culturally acceptable in the happy bubble of the Xmas season.

Invite your next-door neighbor, whom you've only waved to from the driveway for 12 months, out to breakfast at the local diner where you can catch up with her life. If you happen to drop your testimony, she's not likely to push away her ham and eggs and walk out.

Brainstorm Christmas like D-Day. Sometimes a failure to do Christmas right is just a failure of imagination. Ask WWJD questions of yourself and your Christian friends. Find out what "be all things to all men" means. Repent of not believing that the gospel (the Son of God born in a manger, dead for sinners, risen for our salvation) is "the power of God" (1 Corinthians 1:18) that pierces crass commercialism.

THE AFFAIR

*A quiet seed develops—and the
unthinkable becomes thinkable*

SHE CHECKS THE CAR for telltale traces, then
checks it again: a hotel napkin, a book of matches,
an odor. Not that her husband is observant, but as
the saying goes: "For want of a nail, a kingdom is
lost." Most of all, the children must not know.

It is Tuesday afternoon, the usual, pulling in just
ahead of the yellow school bus, sporting the trinkets
they wait for. She prides herself on this—her ability
to manage it all, to not let her mothering slip. She
will shift gears now, give herself entirely to them.
Till Tuesday next, at 1 o'clock. And never the twain
shall meet.

There are times, to be sure, moments only, when
one world veers too close to the other, when the
whole fragile edifice almost comes undone. At
Women's Bible Study (that's Wednesdays) they're
doing "Proverbs," and by chapter 7 she feels a hot

shudder and wonders if it's noticed. A right unpleasant book, that, full of aphorisms that snap shut, boomeranging laws, inflexible as steel and unforgiving as gravity.

Nobody ever wakes up one morning and decides to become an adulteress. You must imagine, rather, Elijah's fist-sized cloud over Mt. Carmel that swells into Ahab's mighty rainstorm. Or the quiet seed gestating in a woman weeks before she even knows she's pregnant. Or, perhaps, a serpent's egg. There appears one day a thought that wasn't there before, a whisper in the heart—of disappointment, discontentment; a vacuum where once abode gratitude. Add the chemistry of idleness and afternoon soaps; the unrelenting barrage of unthinkable suggestions that become, suddenly, thinkable; and your best friend's well-meant counsel: "You deserve better than him."

There is this man at the gym. They talk. His marriage has been failing for some time. He says, "I can really talk to you." She says, "If we had only met when I was free." He says, "I had a dream of you last night." She says, "I am attracted to you too, but it's not right."

Not exactly a slammed door, this. The question is left dangling, the tension is titillating, every weak protest drawing the inevitable closer. Two-tiered messages fly back and forth, careful crafted verbal maneuvers that preserve a moral rectitude but are no defense against the surging undertow. The Rubicon is crossed before flesh ever touches flesh. "For who can carry fire in his lap and not be burned?"

The non-initiate's misunderstanding is that the unfaithful wife has coolly cast off all righteousness. Do not believe it for a second. She has developed her own complicated righteousness, and within its laws and logic is as punctilious as a nun: Faithful to her husband in her own fashion, she rises while it is dark, prepares food for her family, "seeks wool and flax and works with willing hands."

Who is perfect? she thinks. Will not the Blood cover even this? And look, it's been a year and still no sign of divine disapprobation. Surely the Almighty Himself understands her! He knows her needs, that they weren't being met. "God has called you to peace"—says so right in 1 Corinthians 7:15!

Her pastor is a Johnny-one-note preacher. "Flee from sexual immorality!" (1 Corinthians 6:18). "Sin is crouching at the door. Its desire is for you, but you must rule over it" (Genesis 4:7). "Who will deliver me from this body of death? Thanks be to God through Jesus Christ our Lord" (Romans 7:24-25).

She cannot pray, she has tried. ("It is hopeless, for I have loved foreigners, and after them I will go" [Jeremiah 2:25].) If the truth be told, there are days

Andrée Seu

when she is tired. ("You were wearied with the length of your way" [Isaiah 57:10].) "The wicked flee when no one pursues" (Proverbs 28:1)—a Woman's Bible Study verse intrudes from out of the blue as she paints her lips, on a Tuesday at noon. She chuckles (but only barely). "The paranoia of the guilty," she had blurted out on a Wednesday at class, and they all were impressed with her grasp of the Word: "Must be a gift," they cried.

Turning the key in the ignition, she drives away now, thickly scented, to the place she's been a dozen times before. See, nothing evil has befallen me and nothing will, she tells herself, rehearsing all the reasons that she's justified. But all the same she casts a glance behind and to the side, wondering, distractedly, irrationally, if today might be the judgment day.

NOTHING MORE THAN FEELINGS?

*Feelings are fickle and fleeting, but
covenant is faithful and lasting*

THE HEART IS NOT naturally monogamous.

This is the empirical finding of a slightly shopworn middle-aged pilgrim. Among my closest friends are women who are prayer warriors, doers of good deeds, devoted to their husbands—and whose hearts have been drawn anon to another man, to one who stirred·some part of themselves (perhaps an aesthetic temperament) not touched in marriage. It is possible that I need to find better friends. Or perhaps I have merely outgrown fairy tales.

Not much you can do about feelings, I suppose. To be sure, people do things about them all the time: obsess, have affairs, divorce. Some who engage in such remedies have concluded that marriage is a fundamentally flawed concept because it fetters the heart, forcing unnatural impediments. Tarry a while and you will find those philosophers on a street corner panhandling for pocket change with a tin cup, or swelling the welfare rolls as single parents—or tendering resignations, as New Jersey Gov. McGreevey did on Aug. 12, 2004. That is the end of that road.

Gay feelings, straight feelings. Makes no difference, feelings are feelings. I have never met a feeling that wouldn't be a god if you let it. But here is no enduring stuff on which to build a life. Speaking of Eros, C.S. Lewis once said, "She herself is a mocking, mischievous spirit, far more elf than deity, and makes game of us" (*The Four Loves*). He goes on to counsel that "even for their own sakes the loves must submit to be second things if they are to remain the things they want to be. In this yoke lies their true freedom." This advice is worth heeding because "left to themselves [feelings] either vanish or become demons."

Enter the usefulness of covenant.

How does a godly woman keep her way? She takes her feelings to Scripture to have them named. She finds there a framework for her experience: Some yearnings are blessed and others censured. She encounters the ancient phenomenon of covenant, an insight as deep as the dawn of creation and in accord with reality. It takes into account a fact of human existence that fools ignore to their peril—that life is lived out in the matrix of time, in a succession of moments. And therefore, living is marked by inconstancy of feelings, feelings that would threaten to pull asunder by centrifugal force if not brought into submission to a higher rule. The woman now sees her impulses in the light of new possibilities: Not all feelings are friends.

In the same Scriptures she finds remedies. What do you do to rob the oxygen of an illicit ardor? You pray for the man (let's say it is a man) you are attracted to. You pray for his sanctification. You pray for his wife! (This, friends, is a real non-starter for romantic adventurism.) Rather than stoking ungodly feelings till they crescendo to a convincing claim of defining your essence, the tempted woman "sues for grace" (as the Puritans used to say), until the impulses threatening her very soul abate.

Job said, "I have made a covenant with my eyes; how then could I gaze at a virgin?" (Job 31:1). The godly woman likewise makes covenant to treat younger men like brothers, older men like fathers, in all purity (1 Timothy 5:1-2)—which is doable because God Himself keeps covenant. "I will henceforth practice thinking of Mr. X as my blood sibling," she determines, by God's grace. The homosexually inclined man who wants to seek the Lord covenants likewise: "I will henceforth think of Mr. X as my brother."

The struggler with biblically forbidden affections is thereby greatly helped. Now she has something to "put on" as she has had to "put off" unholy things. And in contrast to the world around her where increasingly "the people cast off restraint" (Proverbs 29:18), and mock covenant, she comes to see that covenant is not the problem; it is the solution. Where feelings were fickle tyrants, covenant is a gentle yoke and dependable master, leading her to safe harbors.

Life handed Gov. McGreevey a choice between feelings and covenant, and he went with feelings. The twice-married man chucked his marriage, his governorship, and his life for a tryst with a male aide, declaring, "I am a gay American." Some are calling him "courageous."

As for me and my circle of lady friends, however, because life is not tidy, we hold each other's feet to the covenant. It tides us over the thin patches of feelings, till the day we all come to full sight. We rejoice in covenants at the marriage altar, and those by which we bind ourselves to God, and the one by which our covenant Lord has bound Himself to us.

SIMPLE FAITH

A widowed writer does something highly unusual:
She takes God at His Word

THERE WERE ABOUT FIVE MINUTES of new widowhood when I grasped that I was now in a special demographic where eyes would be on me watching to see God glorified in my circumstances. There was the blinking of an eye when I saw opportunity—a stage for God's "power in weakness" show, a chance to prove Satan wrong in wagering that God's children serve Him only when they're ahead of the game (Job 1). But then I receded again into the pursuit of minimum Christianity: saved by the blood, but entitled to grouse.

I don't outright grouse, not usually. I am sanctified about it—just a well-placed sigh in certain company, just a being "honest" about loneliness. Or, I say nothing at all, either bad or good. If I have known some private comfort in my prayer closet, I never let on, so nobody ever knows it. There's a lyric in the songs my mother used to play in the Frank

Sinatra–Robert Goulet 33 LP pity-party days that said something like "happy to be miserable over you." This is the idea.

Now I have received a book in the mail by a widow writing on widowhood: *He Said, "Press,"* by Patti McCarthy Broderick. Let me say that I never read books about widowhood or the Christian life by people whose day job is housewife. I like books by lettered authors with titles like *The Twentieth Century* or *Postmodernism.* Leave me alone with my personal life. Let's talk epic themes. But I promised I would read it so I did.

Gnosticism is thought to be a dead church issue: A clique of second- to fourth-century guys thought the writings of Paul were quaint, and good enough for the Christian rabble, but for themselves were superseded by a secret inside track to God through mystical channels far more sophisticated than obedience to Christ's simple commands.

Patti Broderick has written a very simple book about her journey. She cites verses like the following and makes much of them:

"I know that you can do all things . . ." (Job 42:2). "Consider the lilies, how they grow . . ." (Luke 12:27). This happened "to make us rely not on ourselves but on God . . ." (2 Corinthians 1:9). "His divine power has granted to us all things that pertain to life and godliness . . ." (2 Peter 1:3).

Ms. Broderick figures that when the Bible says "suffering produces character and character, hope," it means that suffering produces character and character, hope. I, on the other hand, have interposed a baroque system of hermeneutics between the Bible and my life. I have seminary training. Unlike simple people who obey the Bible because they don't realize how complicated it is, I find ambiguity in every verse. I don't obey Scripture, I discuss it.

Patti Broderick and I, at the crossroads of our respective widowhood, evidently heard the same statistics and psychological findings regarding the "natural" course of grief and the amount of time needed to "process" it. I went with the statistics and gave myself permission to be as bad as I wanted to be. She, more simpleminded, files the following report: "So I chose, instead, to bank my life on Scripture being true, and I was not going to let even well-meaning Christians talk me out of it." In this she cites as fixed anchors for the soul such meditations as the following:

"For I know the plans I have for you, declares the Lord, plans for wholeness and not for evil, to give you a future and a hope. Then you will call upon me and come and pray to me, and I will hear you. You will seek me and find me. When you seek me with all your heart, I will be found by you, declares the

Lord, and I will restore your fortunes and gather you from all the nations and all the places where I have driven you, declares the Lord, and I will bring you back to the place from which I sent you into exile." (Jeremiah 29:11-14).

In her simpleminded faith, Patti Broderick decided early on, on the basis of such verses as the one above, that she should make an effort to pray and read the Bible more in order to know God better, blithely unmindful of any problematic taint of legalism in that endeavor. She also studied the lives of Abraham and other Hebrews 11 people and, astoundingly, drew motivation from them to imitate their lives of faith.

That is, Ms. Broderick did the very thing that a Gnostic knows not to do: She took the Bible as practical.

They say "write what you know," and I know widowhood. And I can tell you with assurance that what Patti McCarthy Broderick has done is not natural. The default mode of widowhood is not what she has lived. As the author of this fine book has admitted, she made a conscious choice to trust in God, to take His Word as truth, to see opportunity, and to wear His praises publicly on her lips. And she did not find Him disappointing.

BEHOLD THE MAN

*Birth is not a privilege to withhold from
the cart-man or the carpenter*

ERIK IN MY CHURCH is 23 and has a bent of mind that puts him just outside the spectrum we call "normal." Whatever it is in reality (the angels know), here on the ground the label is autism. Erik has mastered the vital statistics of most everyone in our 1,000-member congregation—the number of kids, their names and ages and where they go to school, their former church affiliations.

The young man also puts in 40 hours a week at a supermarket where I shop, retrieving renegade carts from the lot and corralling them into their pens, in rain or shine or sleet, around the year. He is the first face of Genuardi's for the harried patron seeking milk and eggs and a general good-will feeling.

I commended him on this recently: "People must like you, Erik; you're so friendly to everyone."

"Yes they do, Mrs. Seu," he said (with characteristic absence of false humility).

But then, as I tarried, the stories tumbled out matter-of-factly, anecdotes of minute-long encounters, a biblical resonance to each. Listening, I learn a lesson about winnowing, the teasing out of grain and chaff, on the humble instrument of the cart-man's greetings.

For part of the inflexibility of Erik's condition is a lack of "sophistication" in toning up or down the gospel message, which he lavishes on one and all with admirable democracy. If God shows no partiality, neither does His servant Erik. "How are you, Erik?" "Having a blessed day, Mr. Jones, how about you? Glad to be saved by the grace of Jesus." One group will respond in kind, happy to swap blessings with a fellow pilgrim. One group will walk a bit more briskly by. And then there has been more than one woman, he told me, who will look him straight in the face and shout, F-you!

Jesus of Nazareth had a condition that put Him outside the spectrum of normal in the ancient Near East—of questionable parentage (as the local scuttlebutt went); as likely to welcome a prostitute as chide her; as likely to heal the son of a centurion as that of a Jewish scribe. A challenge to credulity if you've been reading your Torah selectively and self-servingly.

All eyes are fixed on the specimen, scarcely a man

at all, staggering into the moonlight, swaying, spittle-covered, bloodied, the object of recoil and disgust. "His appearance was so marred, beyond human semblance, and his form beyond that of the children of mankind." (Isaiah 52:14). And Pilate, saying far more than he knows, announces, "Behold the man!" (John 19:5). "Ecce Homo!"

"What is man?" Psalm 8 asks. What is the essence of true humanity? "Adam" means "the man," and for a moment of time in Eden, in this First Man was contained the totality of what man was—the federal headship of a category of one. Like Michelangelo's David I picture him—free of blemish, excellent in beauty that we should desire him, and, briefly, unacquainted with suffering of any kind.

There was another garden (and this is no accident). And here our Second Man sweat drops of blood—every inch a king, more master of this garden than ever was His predecessor. Question to ponder: Can it be that Adam the First, Adam the David of Florence, Adam the man-at-ease, is actually the incomplete and embryonic form of personhood? Can it be that Man only reaches his apogee (paradoxically) as a species in man-as-suffering-servant?

In today's world it is demanded that a man "amount to something." And we have a pretty way of defining that. And a pretty way of punishing the falling short of it. Birth is the privilege of those who promise to make our lives "nice" and add to the GNP.

Erik, like Jesus, does not do "nice." But a day is coming when I will meet Erik, and not in the lot at Genuardi's. And I should not be surprised if he walks up to me and says, "Well, Andrée, I am glad God gave me the opportunity to glorify Him with my autism back then—and I am glad it's over now!" And then he shall probably say, before I have a chance, "I was a good and faithful servant." Because Erik never did have false humility.

IRRITATING LOVE

*So many bail the marriage boat because
it's overweighted*

GROUCHO MARX ON LOVE: "Everyone says 'I love you,' though just what they said it for I never knew. It's just inviting trouble for the poor sucker who says 'I love you'" (*Horsefeathers*, 1930).

Paul on love: "Love is patient and kind; love does not envy or boast; it is not arrogant or rude. It does not insist on its own way; it is not irritable or resentful; it does not rejoice at wrongdoing, but rejoices with the truth. Love bears all things, believes all things, hopes all things, endures all things" (1 Corinthians 13, A.D. 70).

There you have it: Groucho and Paul agreeing on love and trouble. Who needs to be "patient" or "kind" where there is no one testing patience or kindness? Why exhort against being "irritable" if there are no irritating elements around? What is there to "bear" where the beloved is eminently lovable, or "believe" where there is no risk in trusting, or "hope" where relationship is already perfected?

But Groucho's question is a valid one. Why say "I love you" if this is how it is? "If such is the case of a man with his wife, it is better not to marry," said the disciples (Matthew 19:10), punctuating with an audible "Phew!" The Lord, not arguing the point, replied, "Not everyone can receive this saying." Consequently, men through the ages (those not made eunuchs for the kingdom of God) persist in a custom that Groucho holds to ridicule, as he reclines in his rowboat and strums idly on strings.

Little wonder the hip-hop generation has cold feet. Statistics portend that half the *I love you*s pronounced at the altar will end in *poor sucker* songs and a bailing out of the boat. That makes the big story here not that so many are choosing to forgo marriage but that so many are marrying in spite of casino odds. It can't all be for "two-for-one meal coupons and discounted health club memberships," as one magazine put it. We evidently want intimacy and commitment.

Since marriage is not going away, then, despite the trouble it invites (cf. Groucho and 1 Corinthians 7:28), let us not enter in willy-nilly. A king at war with another king is thought foolish if he does "not sit down first and deliberate whether" he has the resources for it (Luke 14:31). And Lord knows we have lost more good men and women to badly prepared marriages than badly prepared wars. A few words of advice from someone who's "been there" but not necessarily "done that," (A friend once said, "Nobody's useless: You can always be a bad example."):

First, visualize a triangle. You and your partner at the two lateral angles, God at the top angle. These are the three persons in your marriage. But God is your main relationship. The main one you talk to.

The main one you get life from. The person across the kitchen table (and the triangle) from you, being both a sinner and finite, can never be your finally sufficient relationship. Reckon with this. As Francis Schaeffer writes in *True Spirituality*: "The trouble with human relationships is that man without God does not realize that all men are sinful, and so he hangs too much on his personal relationships, and they crush and break."

Second, the above advice is useless pious sentiment unless rehearsed on a regular basis. The reason is purely mathematical, I would say: The world hammers at you every day, and if you do not combat it every day with truth—that God, and not your mate, is the source of all your good, that He rewards the righteous and those who wait for Him—then worldly wisdom will soon come to look vivid, and the truth will seem thin and unreal. I know a woman who framed her marriage vows on the wall and rereads them every morning lest she forget.

What liberation! What freedom to discover that when we unburden marriage of impossible freight, when we see our spouses correctly as fellow and fallible creatures, we can enjoy what is beautiful in marriage without needing it to be perfect. Relationship can be authentic without being everything.

As for the trouble, Groucho, well, there is trouble in the world anyway, married or single. But "take heart," Jesus says, "I have overcome the world" (John 16:33).

PHILADELPHIA STORY

*Reporters miss a shocking scandal in
the City of Brotherly Love*

THIS ONE ISN'T FOR CHILDREN—although there's bitter irony in the prohibition. The story elements are a hammer, a hatchet, a brick, adolescent treachery, the Supreme Court, and a scandal finale.

In 2003 a girl of 15 from a blue-collar neighborhood just north of the historic district of the City of Brotherly Love enticed a boy into the spit of woods between I-95 and the Delaware River with the promise of sex. Waiting in ambush were the 16-year-old boy's best friend and two other guys, none yet 18. It was Friday and the "young man lacking sense" (Proverbs 7:7) had just got paid, having worked a construction job with his father. He followed the girl, "as an ox goes to the slaughter, or as a stag is caught fast till an arrow pierces its liver; as a bird rushes into a snare; he does not know that it will cost him his life" (Proverbs 7:22-23).

After the massacre, the quartet engaged in a group hug, congratulated themselves, divvied up the contents of the wallet—the princely sum of $500—and copped a few days' worth of heroin, marijuana, and pills. One of the boys later confessed, "We partied beyond redemption."

This isn't the scandal part.

In March of the present year the three boys were given life without parole, just cheating death by a fortuitous confluence of events in which a trial taking place elsewhere in the country got bumped up to the U.S. Supreme Court, which body ruled—with fear and trembling, I hope—against the execution of killers under the age of 18. The seductress (let's call her "Jane," for she comes up again in our tale) was handed a sentence of 17 to 35 years.

Jane penned a jailhouse epistle that read like so: "I'm a cold-blooded [expletive] death-worshipping bitch who survives by feeding off the weak and lonely. I lure them, and then I crush them."

But this isn't the scandal either.

You may be reminded, presently, of a tale of depravity from the pages of the book of Judges, told with chilling matter-of-factness. The elements here are a feckless Levite, his concubine, a town without pity, and body parts scattered unceremoniously to the four corners of Israel; and the purpose of the telling is to illustrate the depths of depravity where the knowledge of God is lost in the land. But don't chase down that rabbit hole; that's not where I'm going with this yarn—and it's not the scandal either.

I happened to ask my 23-year-old (she is not a believer; she is familiar with the neighborhood in question) if she'd been following the case, and Hae Linn said no but that she knew Jane's elder sister. The only other information I got out of her is that the elder sister says she's been getting letters from Jane and "they're full of Jesus."

Your call, reader. This coda to the tale (don't look for it in the *Inquirer*) is whispered down the lane, as it were. Reliable as water-cooler talk, maybe. But if it's true, if Jane's letters home are now "full of Jesus," then this is the scandal I've been promising you. This is the kicker, the O'Henry twist in the plot.

C.S. Lewis tells in *The Great Divorce* of an encounter on the threshold of heaven between a murderer now gloriously sanctified and a tourist from hell. The day visitor is indignant to find the murderer in Paradise. The heavenly citizen explains to him, "Murdering old Jack wasn't the worst thing I did. That was the work of a moment and I was half mad when I did it. But I murdered you in my heart, deliberately, for years."

Unmoved, the tourist stands on his decent earthly

record and snarls, "I'm not asking for anybody's bleeding charity." "Then do. At once," replies the Shining one. "Ask for the Bleeding Charity. Everything here is for the asking and nothing can be bought."

It's the gospel scandal. "Amazing grace, how sweet the sound that saved a wretch like me." Now and then we are reminded how amazing it is.

MENTAL FILIBUSTERS

*When obsessing over theology becomes
a way to avoid obedience*

CAROLYN DID GREEK BOOT CAMP with me at seminary. She was a Carolinian, a people person, and outspoken in her love for Jesus—everything I was not. I chalked it up to Southern culture. I explained to her that I was reticent by natural endowment, and more prone to wait for the right moment. She wasn't impressed: "I've got plenty of faults, but shuttin' up ain't one of them."

I did not like Carolyn.

Twenty-seven-odd years later I'm still waiting for the right moment, and Carolyn's probably blabbed the gospel all over Dixie. She has offended many people, I'm sure. A few have come to faith (law of averages). She has done this though I'll bet dollars to donuts I scored higher in Apologetics. I, on the other hand, continue to be culturally sensitive. No neighbor of mine can fault me for violating boundaries after 18 years on the block. I have tiptoed over with homemade cream puffs, and tomatoes from my garden, without them ever suspecting I did it for Christ.

Carolyn probably has no idea how many places there are to get waylaid along Professor Clowney's rectangular grid that takes you from the Hebrew data, to the original meaning for the ancient Near Eastern audiences, to the Christological meaning, to contemporary cultural application. She does not lose sleep over whether women should don a head covering in church, or other vexing questions touching on contextualization, continuity versus discontinuity, biblical-historical dispensations (small "d"), and linguistics. She forges ahead.

From my catbird seat at the café I see two kinds of seminary students—the Carolyns and the "yours truly" variety. The latter linger long over coffee and go a few rounds of theology, weighing, nuancing, balancing, finessing, finding the philosophical fly in the ointment, finally leaving with matters unresolved but a good time had by all. They throw up their hands and say that God's commands are uncertain, and subject to interpretation; perhaps we will understand them by and by.

Here's something I would never have done: One of the new students and his family, folks from Peru, arrived on a shoestring and landed in the apartment just over that of my parents. Miguel for a while was in the humbling position of begging rides off my mother (not a Christian) for every little thing. On one such day, as they returned from an errand, Miguel turned to my mom and thanked her for all her help, then added: "But you realize, don't you, that none of it will get you into heaven."

Bravo, Miguel, for not bogging down in "Who is my neighbor?" and other mental filibusters. Bravo, Dietrich Bonhoeffer, for paying the supreme price for a life of faith rather than abstraction. "We have literally no time to sit down and ask ourselves whether so-and-so is our neighbor or not," wrote the German pastor executed by Nazis weeks before war's end. The rich young man "had hoped to avoid committing himself to any definite moral obligations by forcing Jesus to discuss his spiritual problems. . . . Only the devil has an answer for our moral difficulties, and he says, 'Keep on posing problems, and you will escape the necessity of obedience'" (*The Cost of Discipleship*).

It's May, exam time at the seminary. School alert: Consider the insidiousness of slipping away from Christ while you're studying Christ—seeing 10:30 Chapel as optional, library research as the lifeline. "There have been men before now who got so interested in proving the existence of God that they came to care nothing for God Himself . . . as if the good Lord had nothing to do but exist! There have been some who were so occupied in spreading Christianity that they never gave a thought to Christ. . . . It is the subtlest of all the snares" (*The Great Divorce*).

I am falling in love with Jesus today where I was just half-heartedly dating before. He said, draw near to Me and I will draw near to you (James 4:8), and I have taken note. Sleepers awake! "All that is over now. We are not playing now. . . . I will bring you to the land not of questions but of answers, and you will see the face of God" (Ibid.).

And I'm starting to like Carolyn better all the time.

SEVENTEEN MINUTES

It's the thoughts—ordinary, daily thoughts—that count

THESE ARE THE THOUGHTS of a woman driving home from the Stop 'N Shop on an ordinary day.

She conjures three comebacks she could've hurled at Ellen if she had not been caught off guard.

She spots the baby shower invitation on the dashboard and schemes a way to be out of town that weekend—then thinks better of it because she has a favor to ask the sender at a later date.

She sizes up a woman standing at the bus stop—and judges her.

She stews over a comment her brother made behind her back, and crafts a letter telling him off—and sounding righteous in the process.

She reviews the morning's argument with her husband, and plans the evening installment.

She imagines how life would have been if she had married X (a well-worn furrow, this).

She magnanimously lets a car merge into traffic,

and then is ticked off when she doesn't get her wave.

She resolves to eat less chocolate starting today—well, tomorrow.

She replays memory tapes going back to the '60s, trying to change the endings.

Somebody rides up the road shoulder and budges to the head of a traffic jam, and she hates the driver with a perfect hatred.

She passes the house of the contractor who defrauded her and fantasizes blowing it to smithereens.

She passes Audrey working in her garden and waves—but thinks, "If Audrey has chronic fatigue syndrome, I'm a Flying Wallenda."

She glares at a driver who runs a red light in front of her, forgetting that she did the same about a mile ago.

She checks her slightly crooked nose compulsively in the rearview mirror, and reassures herself it isn't too bad.

An inner voice tells her to turn off the radio and pray, but she decides that's the voice of legalism.

She brainstorms talking points for her upcoming woman's Bible study lecture on "Ephesians" and considers how she can improve it—and make it better than Alice's talk of last week.

She is angry at God because here she is a Christian and broke, while her good-for-nothing heathen of a brother is rolling in dough.

She thinks how much better her life would be if she were beautiful, and fantasizes all the bungee-jumping, maggot pizza–eating "Fear Factor" stunts she'd be willing to subject herself to to look like Gwyneth Paltrow.

She wonders how her parents will divvy up the inheritance—and how long she has to wait.

She rehearses two good reasons why her sister and not she should take care of the folks when they're too old. She thinks about her childhood and counts the ways her parents have screwed up her life.

The Johnsons drive by, and she recalls all the meals she made for them 10 years ago when Lydia had toxemia during pregnancy, and bets they don't even remember. Hmm, did they even send a thank-you card?

The word *treachery* flashes through her mind (Mr. Beaver's succinct epithet for Edmund in *The Lion, the Witch, and the Wardrobe*) but leaves no footprints.

An SUV cuts her off, and she decides to punish it by tailgating.

Her heart smites her for this. So she determines to try harder to live righteously from now on. Who knows, God may reward her in some amazing way: Her husband may give her grounds for divorce, and

God will lead her to the arms of Mr. Right.

She tries to pray but doesn't get past "Our Father."

There are lots of other people that the woman does not think of while driving home with groceries, people who are not important to her social status, or just not interesting.

She doesn't think about AIDS-ravaged Africa, she doesn't think about the death sentence dangling over millions in Sudan, she doesn't think about missionaries, she doesn't think about martyrs in Kim Jong-il's prisons, she doesn't think about ways she could encourage her children.

She pulls into her driveway. Total driving time: 17 minutes.

And if you were to ask the lady, as she rustles parcels from the car, what she has been thinking about on the drive from town, she would say, "Oh, nothing in particular." And she would not be lying.

Imagine believing that we don't need a Savior.

JOYFUL FANATICS

———————•———————

Is it good to become beside ourselves for Christ?

I HAVEN'T BEEN MYSELF LATELY. A chain of events whose recounting is not appropriate for this page unsettled temporarily the contented stagnant waters of my heart, making a return to torpid pools unthinkable.

Here is a question for you: Is it possible to be too excited about Jesus? (Are you personally in any danger of that?) Possible to go off the deep end and think about Him overmuch? To rejoice beyond propriety? To talk about Him as freely as about a football game? To have an almost giddy confidence in what He will do next? To fast and pray for deeper life with Him? To be overly preoccupied with evangelism?

I am on the verge of wanting to hang out with people I used to dismiss as fanatics. Now a fanatic, of course, is anyone on that great bandwidth of Christian experience who talks about Jesus more than you do—your own position being counted the sensible standard. So, for example, on one end would be the Christian-Democratic parties of Europe that most reading this magazine would not even recognize as Christian (all that remains is the name, the smile on the Cheshire cat). On the other end would be, well, Paul the apostle, "beside himself" for Christ (2 Corinthians 5:13), being lowered in baskets from walls, and such.

Between teems an endlessly subdivided landscape. There are Christians who talk about God in church, but would never at a party. There are Christians who pray in church but would never in your kitchen. Some will drop and pray right there between fridge and microwave. (I remember my first kitchen praying experience; it was 22 years ago with a woman named Audrey L., who judged that our conversation had reached a point where immediate intercession with Christ was in order. I thought her quite . . . fanatical.) Making one's way in any culture becomes, as far as that goes, a matter of understanding what is appropriate behavior in the group you find yourself in, whether they are the church-and-kitchen praying kind of people or just the within-the-nave praying kind of people.

Now I have been a Christian for a long time, even a kitchen type. So I always fancied myself at the extreme right of the spectrum (that is, opposite the

European political Christians), all other shades of Christianity sloping off to my side in their myriad shades of perfidy.

Along comes R.R., and he has joy like a fire hose. Letters comes to my door, page after page fairly bristling in my hand for uncontainable elation— what Jesus has done for him, is now doing, was certain to do. He is the demoniac of the Gadarenes now "dressed and in his right mind." He is Mary Magdalene, loving much because he's been forgiven much. He reads Scripture greedily, and like you read your girlfriend's letters.

Because I never had real joy, I'd learned to redefine "joy" in the Bible as an abstraction. Because I had no real faith, I took "faith" in the Bible as poetic, metaphorical. I had no real "abundant life" to speak of, and so was forced to make the term a figure of speech.

The optometrist has a contraption in his office with a series of graduated lenses through which you read the wall chart. Lens A seems good to you at first, but then he tries Lens B and it's a better fit. You had not yet seen as clearly as you could.

There have always been joyful Christians vaguely fluttering around me, those baffling folks on the fringes of my consciousness who count it fun to sing their gospel songs and show no interest in the depressing ballads that I favor. They never were my cup of tea. But like I said, I haven't been myself lately. I'm tasting promissory notes of joy in Christ. Scriptures long frozen like wax figures at Madame Tussaud's are warming to life.

Is this sanity or fanaticism? Let Scripture be the plumb line. "Though you do not now see him, you believe in him and rejoice with joy that is inexpressible and filled with glory" (1 Peter 1:8). Try overdoing this verse if you can.

ASK, RECEIVE, DISBELIEVE?

No, God spared me the death sentence: praise to Him alone

DR. GREENBERG FOUND A LUMP. A "thickening," she called it, and with professional sangfroid, jotted on my chart. Trained fingertips—2,000 receptors per digit and sensitive to a dot 3 microns high (the diameter of a human hair is 50 to 100 microns), or to textures 75 nanometers deep (one-thousandth the diameter of a human hair)—were the bearers of bad news. Let evolutionists despair and intelligent designers delight: The most advanced robotic "fingers" engineered by man are clumsy with the toddler's task of picking up a drinking glass.

"All men live under a sentence of death. They all go sooner or later. But I'm different. I have to go at 6 a.m. tomorrow morning. It would have been 5, but I had a good lawyer" (Woody Allen as peasant Boris, soon to face a firing squad in *Love and Death*). Not so funny anymore. Not funny either when moments later in her private office, my new nemesis says,

"When you phone for the mammogram, tell them to put you at the head of the class."

History-changing upheavals walk in small and unimpressive: a snatch of tape spied by a lonely night watchman at the Watergate complex; the word *thickening* barely breathed into the ether. The universe is irreversibly altered. There is a chasm fixed, with me on one side and 6 billion people on the other, their comings and goings a blur of absurd commotion. "Then two men will be in the field; one will be taken and one left. Two women will be grinding at the mill; one will be taken and one left." No lover's bond, no cable of motherly devotion to her child, no ardency of friendship, will revoke the ripping apart.

That was the first morning. At evening I called Ronnie, my most violent friend. "Violent" in the sense of C.H. Spurgeon, who wrote, "'The kingdom of heaven suffereth violence, and the violent take it by force.' But this violence does not end when a man finds Christ; it then begins to exercise itself in another way. . . . Mark such a man who is a true Christian, mark his prayers, and you will see there is violence in all his supplications." So Ronnie supplicated violently over this sister, and I went to bed.

The following I report without commentary, in the manner of Luke's restrained report of the miraculous rescue of Peter in answer to prayer, where the prayer warriors on hearing of it said to Rhoda, "You are out of your mind." I was put to the head of the class. I was mammogrammed and ultrasounded and prodded with professional fingers—and totally exonerated of my death sentence.

Now when do you have a certifiable miracle? Well, never, if you claim *a priori* that miracles have ceased. And never if, like me, your mind leaps like a duck on a June bug to naturalistic explanation: Doctor A blew it. The latter theory is possible, of course, but on the other hand, what would it take, and how much proof, before I acknowledged the supernatural in my life? (Father Abraham says even raising a corpse wouldn't do it for folks of a certain ilk. Luke 16:31.) Francis Schaeffer draws the line precisely here between the Christian mind and the non-Christian mind: "I am not a Bible-believing Christian in the fullest sense simply by believing the right doctrines, but as I live in practice in this supernatural world" (*True Spirituality*).

My violent intercessor seems to think that since we prayed watchfully (Colossians 4:2), and since the request we sought was granted, it's a no-brainer that I need to give public glory to God. There are precedents, of course: The leper is healed and forthwith told by Jesus to go show himself to the priest (Matthew 8:4). Still I protested vainly: "Many godly people pray and are not healed." Violent replied, "You were. Shout it from the housetops"—plus words to the effect that it's a dangerous thing to ask the Almighty for something, and then, having received it, to flirt with unbelief. There was no gainsaying that, and in the end I saw the truth of it, and yielded doubt to faith, and that is why I tell you this.

So here receive my public thanks to God. To Him alone be praise.

HOUSE OF UNRAVELING

*A storm sent to demolish my building
materials and establish my trust*

THE UNRAVELING OF SHYLOCK'S life in *The Merchant of Venice* is as painful a story denouement as has ever been depicted. It is the account of the removal, one at a time, in rapid succession, of everything Shylock held fast to for life.

He leaves home one evening with his daughter, his ducats, and his dignity intact. He returns to find his daughter has eloped—to the enemy's side. More, she has absconded with his ducats as a dowry. Reeling and staggering, he cannot take in the enormity of his misfortune: from wealth to woe in 24 hours. "Oh my ducats, my daughter. My ducats, my daughter," he moans like a man concussed.

What he has left in the world is his vengeance, which he nurses and cherishes like a beloved pet lizard. But lo, another striptease of soul awaits him before the Duke of Venice. The hellish pleasure that remains to vindictive Shylock is extracting his pound of flesh, yet he loses his legal case and in final ignominy has the tables turned so that he himself becomes the groveling debtor to his nemesis.

Shakespeare does not explicitly say so at this point—it is not necessary—but Shylock will die shortly hereafter, either by his own hand or by the simple inability of his heart to beat.

Call me Shylock. I write as one freshly dismantled. Again. Thought I had my house set on the Rock this time 100 percent. Maybe it was only 50 or 60. Was cruising, gaining altitude, some self-styled Amelia Earhart in a Lockheed Vega, not noticing that the coordinates had drifted. God is in the business of bringing one's trusts to light, of pulling rugs of our own making from under our feet.

It's all good. The alternative is the houses C.S. Lewis described in *The Great Divorce*, which our protagonist finds himself discussing on a rainy evening that never advances to night. He meets the Intelligent Man, who says: "The trouble is they have no Needs. You get everything you want (not very good quality, of course) by just imagining it." (The Intelligent Man is a capitalist and sees a chance to introduce some real commodities and cash in.)

"But look here," asks the bewildered newcomer, "if they can get everything just by imagining it, why would they want any real things, as you call them?" "Eh? Oh well, they'd like houses that really kept out the rain." "Their present houses don't?" "Well of course not. How could they?" "What the devil is the use of building them, then?" "Safety again," the I.M. mutters. "At least the feeling of safety. It's all right now; but later on . . . you understand." "What?" asks the protagonist. The I.M. leans and whispers: "It will be dark presently."

Tim Keller, pastor of Redeemer Presbyterian Church in Manhattan, said, "People won't come to Christ unless they have nothing—and most people don't have that." Amen. I myself have never come to Christ when I had something—never mind that the somethings have been imaginary houses and imaginary assets. As C.S. Lewis says, "There is always something they prefer to joy—that is, to reality."

Given half a chance, would I not, even now, revert like Faust to every life prop but Jesus, though I knew it to be choosing unreality? The question is moot. He does not allow. He sends the storm and exposes—yea, demolishes—my building materials. Nothing now remains but Christ, no good but Him, no possession but Him, no confidence but Him. I choose Him by default—and incredibly He accepts that. Thou meekest divine suitor of my soul, You take me back again.

I am not Shylock after all. I am a daughter of the King and He has set His love on me. You will catch me in Your everlasting arms as I embrace the freefall of a perfect trust in You. When will I learn to trust You more? The night comes on, when those who build on emptiness will groan. C.S. Lewis: "Overcome us that, so overcome, we may be ourselves: We desire the beginning of Your reign as we desire dawn and dew, wetness at the birth of light."

THE NEXT THING

*Why fear the future when the future
belongs only to God?*

I BAGGED RICE ON a co-op line elbow-to-elbow with a peaceful woman who was the mother of nine children by birth and adoption, and was involved in the pro-life movement. I asked how she did it, and to her credit she didn't brush off the question with feigned modesty, but said, "I do the next thing that needs to be done."

I have pondered that statement for years, the distillation of a lady's life of wisdom. Sue is a Christian, so I know what lay unspoken in her answer: First, God is sovereign; second God is good. Indeed, it cannot be otherwise if one would simply "do the next thing that needs to be done."

First, if God were not in perfect control, Sue would have to control all things, even every atom in the universe, to assure a desirable outcome. But she knows she cannot in fact control all things, not even the next two minutes, and so she concedes control to Him.

Second, she believes that the God who controls all things controls them for her good (Romans 8:28). On these twin pillars does her soul find rest.

Sue's Bible also contains commands, rules to live by. And so, what Sue has done, evidently, is to divide life into two categories: the things she can and must do something about, and the things she cannot and must not, for they belong to God (Deuteronomy 29:29).

Mary the mother of Jesus was hep to that division of labor. She "did the next thing" during an awkward wedding moment. Being lousy at making water into wine, she turned to her Son and said, "They have no wine," then went on her merry way to do whatever it was she was able to do herself—folding tablecloths or stalling thirsty guests. Jesus, not one to turn down people who come to Him for help while acknowledging their own helplessness, performed the harder part.

Am I too busy these days? Discouraged over duties left undone? I will preach to myself that there is only one priority—the glory of God—and under that the several duties. When these come flying fast and thick, I will do triage and decide what should come "next." It's God's problem, not mine, to orchestrate the universe and make it all pan out.

Am I fearful? Fear is a focus on phantoms of the theoretical future. But the future is God's, not mine; mine is only the present moment. I am fearful because I'm thinking I have to live the rest of my life. But I don't. I only have to live the next five minutes. To me belongs obedience; to Him belongs outcomes.

We have so far discussed in general terms. But life does not throw up "general terms"; it throws up brutal concreteness: No one's been fed dinner; Aimée is having a sixth-grade crisis; the roof leaks; unread newspapers pile up like an indictment. I will review what I know of God, and do "the next thing." His job is making it all work.

Am I depressed? The concept of doing "the next thing" is just the ticket. Granted, I am far too weak to go on with life—but I can do a load of laundry. And after that I can make the kids breakfast. And after that I can pick up the phone and call a deacon for help on balancing that checkbook. One foot in front of the other: Do "the next thing."

Have I totally messed up my life? Fine, make a list. Here are the things I cannot do: I cannot turn back the clock, I cannot cork up sinful words once spoken, I cannot take back squandered opportunities in career or love. But here are things I can do: I can start from today—with today's time, today's skills, today's health, today's grace. I can do this trusting, even at this stage of the game, that God is still sovereign and still good. And faith, come to think of it, is the whole enchilada.

The lady at the co-op was a well-placed prophet. And said it more succinctly than this writer could.

*

GOING HOME

Lessons learned on the road of life

I WENT HOME RECENTLY and found out that everything you need to know about life can be learned on the stretch of road between Willow Grove, Pa., and Woonsocket, R.I. This is scarcely strange since not only is life like a journey, with a beginning and end, but everything in creation is a metaphor in some way.

For starters, Christians always travel in fundamentally hospitable terrain since we are always in our Father's world. The trees that streak past my window are all His. (Narnia notwithstanding, none have gone over to the White Witch's side.)

Moreover, I can look at the trees and say, "Ah, yes, I know what you are. There are men who can tell better than I about your phylogeny and photosynthesis and capillary action, but they have said nothing true about the tree until they know by Whom a tree comes. I, Christian traveler, know "treeness.""

On the New Jersey Turnpike I exceed the speed limit like everyone else. The signs say 65; my speedometer hovers at 72. I, Christian traveler, want to justify myself—"have to keep up with the flow"— but I feel a discomfort, a fissure of reason and truth. And a suspicion that the deliberate undermining of a particular law tends, like a spreading ink blot, to the disdain of all law.

On the Cross Bronx Expressway, every speedo-meter, the righteous and the unrighteous, plunges to 5 mph—though I had timed this trip to avoid New York City rush hour, and it is well past 7 p.m. Anyone who believes a person's private choices are his own business has never been part of a grounded caravan of several hundred cars with their destinies altered by a "private" choice about two miles up the road. The cause becomes clear half an hour later: Bronco carcass in the passing lane, spun around like a toy so it faces the wrong direction; another crumpled vehicle at some distance. Perhaps the Bronco was racing to a Rangers game; perhaps the other was headed home to see the folks, like me. Appointments never to be kept: "on that very day his plans perish" (Psalm 146:4)

The scene also instructs me that "the race is not to the swift . . . but time and chance happen to them all" (Ecclesiastes 9:11). "Chance," of course, is the perspective "under the sun"; The Christian traveler, the one who knows trees, knows something of the sovereignty of God.

And knows all men, too. Wherever I roam, even if to "deepest, darkest Africa," I can know something significantly true of every man I meet right off the bat. There was a time when I had no idea of this. In my locust-eaten years without God, when everything was possible, it was possible that the next person to walk up to me was something new in the universe— a being perfect, sinless, the direct channel to mystical enlightenment. Or a force outside God's sphere of knowledge.

Near Darien, Conn., I stop for gas. I look at the man pumping petrol next to me and know: Here is a most wonderful creature, an image-bearer of God. And, of course, a sinner too.

That sinner, I note with interest, is not sticking me up for the contents of my wallet, though it is night, he is large, and I am alone with two sleeping kids— easy pickings. Nor has the teenage boy who handed me my Kids' Meal at the Drive-thru spit in my fries, though he will never see me again, so why not.

I meditate on "common grace" and how although men are totally depraved they are not absolutely depraved. Paul is right: The Spirit restrains the world from being as corrupt as it could be (2 Thessalonians 2:7).

When I arrive home—or is Pennsylvania home?—the lesson, alas, is the same I learned last year, and the year before: that all earthly homes produce as much longing as satisfaction, are signposts and not the city itself. And I thank God both for the foretaste and the vague yearning that keeps me headed homeward, keeps my heart on pilgrimage.

A NOTE ABOUT THE AUTHOR

Directly influenced by Francis Schaeffer, her time under his teaching at the L'Abri chalet located in the Swiss Alps, and an ex-druggie, ninth-grade dropout friend, Andrée found that becoming a Christian was not a resignation to denial but the door to a garden of grace and peace.

Andrée began writing eighteen years ago after an aspiring writer moved in next door. On the occasion of her daughter's shedding a baby tooth, her neighbor dropped a poem in her mailbox. Andrée cried on the spot at the sheer beauty of it. Encouraged, her young neighbor started writing more and depositing poems, then essays, then short stories on the porch after dark. This "box" tradition continued for a few years and became Andrée's personal school of writing. Beth Kephart went on to be a semi-finalist for the National Book Award.

Andrée Seu lives and writes from Philadelphia and is a senior writer for *WORLD Magazine*.

A NOTE ABOUT THE PUBLISHER

For more than 20 years, *WORLD Magazine* has established itself as the premier weekly newsmagazine written from a Christian worldview. Published weekly except for two biweekly issues, one at year-end and one in July, *WORLD Magazine* reaches an average of 135,000 paid subscribers. Among general weekly newsmagazines, *WORLD Magazine* ranks in the top five behind *TIME, Newsweek, U.S. News & World Report,* and *THE WEEK Magazine. WORLD Magazine* would appreciate your support. Plus *WORLD Magazine* features Andrée Seu's essays.

If you enjoyed this book, then you may enjoy reading Andrée Seu's insights and thoughts published in *WORLD Magazine.* To subscribe, please contact: *WORLD Magazine,* PO Box 20002, Asheville, NC 28802-9883 or call (800) 951-6397. You may also find *WORLD Magazine* online at www.worldmag.com. Be sure to mention the following promotional code when you write or call: WL66ANDR.

Won't Let You Go Unless You Bless Me